PART ONE

INTRODUCTION

HOW TO STUDY A PLAY

Studying on your own requires self-discipline and a carefully thought-out work plan in order to be effective.

- Drama is a special kind of writing (the technical term is **genre**) because it needs a performance in the theatre to arrive at a full interpretation of its meaning. Try to imagine that you are a member of the audience when reading the play. Think about how it could be presented on the stage, not just about the words on the page.

- Drama is always about conflict of some sort (which may be below the surface). Identify the conflicts in the play and you will be close to identifying the large ideas or themes which bind all the parts together.

- Make careful notes on themes, character, plot and any **subplots** of the play.

- Why do you like or dislike the characters in the play? How do your feelings towards them develop and change?

- Playwrights find non-realistic ways of allowing an audience to see into the minds and motives of their characters, for example **soliloquy**, aside or music. Consider how such dramatic devices are used in the play you are studying.

- Think of the playwright writing the play. Why were these particular arrangements of events, characters and speeches chosen?

- Cite exact sources for all quotations, whether from the text itself or from critical commentaries. Wherever possible find your own examples from the play to back up your opinions.

- Always express your ideas in your own words.

This York Note offers an introduction to *Henry IV Part I* and cannot substitute for close reading of the text and the study of secondary sources.

The first readers of this play in 1598 would have seen on its title page the promise of 'The History of Henrie the Fourth, With the battell at Shrewsburie, betweene the King and Lord Henry Percy, surnamed Henrie Hotspur of the North. With the humorous conceits of Sir John Falstaffe'. Battles and **comedy** were the staple materials for the **genre** of the English history play, which had begun to appear on the London stage around a decade before. Shakespeare's play was popular enough not only to produce a sequel on the reign of Henry IV (*Henry IV Part II*), but also an entirely separate spin-off, *The Merry Wives of Windsor* (c.1597), built around Falstaff and other comic characters from both plays transplanted to a contemporary late-Elizabethan setting. Indeed, Falstaff himself was so popular that Shakespeare's *Henry V*, which traces the progress of Prince Hal from the two *Henry IV* plays once he has become Henry V, includes a description of the fat knight's death, even though he does not appear in the play itself. But the play has much more to offer than one exceptional character. Although Falstaff is undoubtedly one of Shakespeare's most memorable creations, audiences and readers since Shakespeare's day have also been drawn to the play as an analysis of politics, honour and the making of royalty.

The title page does not mention Henry's son, Prince Hal, around whom many of these themes coalesce. As well as the elements mentioned above, *Henry IV Part I* is the story of Hal's pursuit of honour, and his movement from the periphery of the political world to its centre. When the play begins, the king's eldest son is in disgrace, spending his time in the tavern rather than at court. He is involved in a robbery, and is seemingly ignorant, or unmindful, of the nationally significant quarrels smouldering elsewhere, in which his own father's legitimacy as king are questioned. By the end of the play, however, Prince Hal has become his father's right-hand man, rescuing him in battle, and challenging and defeating in single combat the main threat to his rule, Harry Percy, the 'Hotspur' mentioned on the 1598 title page. One of the play's concerns is to explore the psychology of such a dramatic change, and to show the gains and losses of the path Hal eventually takes, for in eventually reconciling himself to his father he distances himself from the character who functions in some way as a father-figure – Falstaff. *Henry IV Part I* is thus, amongst other things, the story of Hal's transformation from unruly adolescent to dutiful son.

The concept of honour is crucial to an understanding of both the

CONTENTS

politics of the play and Hal's motivation in changing. The most eloquent spokesman for honour in the play – indeed, its embodiment, for good and ill – is Hotspur. For Hotspur, honour, understood as both reputation and the deeds from which reputation springs, is paramount. Death with honour is preferable to a dishonourable life. Hotspur's enthusiasm, his bravery and his insistence that it is how you live, rather than how long you live, that matters have all endeared him to audiences and readers as well as ensuring that easy judgements on the wrongness of rebellion are difficult to sustain. Hotspur is also important as an example to Prince Hal. They are the same age, but when the play opens Hotspur is universally admired and Hal is an embarrassment to his royal father. When Hal does eventually take his place beside his father and younger brother on the battlefield at Shrewsbury, it is a sign that he now publicly recognises the responsibilities of his position as monarch-in-waiting, and has taken upon himself Hotspur's commitment to not merely live honourably, but be seen to do so.

The battle of Shrewsbury is the culmination of both the political plot and the story of Hal's maturation. But it also sees the (mock) death and (mock) resurrection of the play's most famous character, Falstaff. Throughout the play, Falstaff entertains a small court (Bardolph, the Hostess, Nym and Prince Hal himself) in the tavern at Eastcheap, and in doing so entertains audience and reader also. He is irreverent, quick-witted, boastful, and funny. He lives for the moment – for eating, drinking, pranks and games, and has apparently spent his long life in doing so. Hal must deny the attractions of Falstaff's world in order to attain fully his royal destiny; Falstaff denies himself nothing. As W.H. Auden pointed out, in this he resembles not an old man but an infant, irresponsible and attractive. But Falstaff is not simply an engaging representative of a world rightly debarred from the serious world of politics, comic relief to the serious business of war and government. He goes to war too, and once he has left the relatively cosy world of his tavern in Eastcheap Falstaff turns his considerable intelligence to a critique of the world of honour that Hotspur inhabits and Hal seeks to enter. As more and more meet death in search of honour, he sardonically asks whether it is worth such a sacrifice for something so easily lost. Hal's adoption of the values of his father and the world of honour thus entails a rejection of Falstaff's sceptical intelligence as well as his roguishness.

The title page of the 1598 edition's promise of battles and jokes, though noting the most obviously crowd-pleasing elements, only scratches the surface of this play. The play is blessed with four strong characters – the king, Prince Hal, Hotspur and Falstaff – and through the interactions of these characters, and others, explores complexities of political action, war and growing up from a variety of perspectives, public and private. Critics have divided over these and other issues, often depending on whether they have focused on the play in performance or on the page. As anyone who has seen the play in the theatre will have noted, Falstaff is a much more attractive character in performance than he is on the page, which in turn influences how seriously his lawlessness or the prince's ambivalent relationship with him are seen. Hotspur, too, has attractive qualities – energy, spontaneity, sense of humour – which come through strongly in performance. Critics who wish to interpret the play moralistically – whether in the eighteenth century as a condemnation of Falstaff's 'vice', or in the twentieth as a condemnation of 'rebellion' – often overlook, or have problems coming to terms with, the play in the theatre. For example, laughter is predominantly a social phenomenon – it happens much more often, and more easily, in groups of people than with solitary individuals. Audiences laugh, or cheer, more than readers do. It is easier to condemn Falstaff as a petty criminal, as some critics have done, if you have not laughed with and at him in a theatre.

Though much critical discussion of *Henry IV Part I* links the play into its predecessor and (sometimes more damagingly) its sequel, it is not necessary to have read either *Richard II*, which deals with Henry IV's coming to the throne and his deposition of Richard II, or *Henry IV Part II*, in which Hal finally becomes king and conclusively and finally rejects Falstaff. *Henry IV Part I*, as can be seen from the number of times characters in it recount the events leading to Henry IV becoming king, is not written in the expectation that audience or reader will know the earlier play in detail. Because *Henry IV Part II* features many of the same characters as *Henry IV Part I*, critics often discuss them together. This in turn means that the earlier play is sometimes read too much in the light of the later, more downbeat, one, particularly where Falstaff's and Hal's characters and relationship are concerned (they only spend one scene together). But *Henry IV Part I* is a self-contained play. All you need to know about events 'outside' the play is supplied by the characters themselves.

Y

Henry IV Part I is not only a play, but a history play, a fiction with a relationship with historical fact. Critics have argued over the extent to which the play can be seen to be a serious engagement with the national past, naturally focusing on Shakespeare's inventions, omissions and compressions. Do these changes to Shakespeare's historical sources – and there are many of them – indicate a cavalier attitude to history, merely as a source of plots, to be manipulated purely for dramatic effect? Or, despite the compromises necessary to give dramatic shape to historical events and processes, do they show Shakespeare as an historian, interested in, if not reproduction of the 'raw facts', exploring the larger historical processes which contributed to the creation of the England in which he lived and worked?

PART TWO

SUMMARIES & COMMENTARIES

As with many of Shakespeare's plays, *Henry IV Part I* was published as an individual **quarto** edition close to the date of its first performance, and as part of Shakespeare's collected works after his death in the more expensive **folio** format. Modern editions are based upon the earliest quarto text of the play, which dates from 1598, though they occasionally prefer readings that make more sense from later and slightly different versions of the text. For example, Peter Davison's New Penguin edition (in common with many others) substitutes 'similes' for the 1598 quarto's 'smiles' at Act I Scene 2 line 79. References in this note are to this New Penguin edition, published in 1996.

SYNOPSIS

The play opens with a setback to Henry IV's plans for a crusade, which he has been planning for a year, and with which he hopes to unite an England recently disrupted by his own usurpation of the throne from his predecessor and cousin, Richard II. There have been military setbacks on the Welsh borders, where Mortimer has been captured by the Welsh. In the north, Harry Percy (Hotspur), who has been leading the northern nobility against the Scots, is refusing to give up the prisoners he took at the battle of Holmedon to the king. Henry sends for Hotspur to question him, and postpones the crusade. Meanwhile, away from the court, Henry's eldest son Hal is amusing himself with Sir John Falstaff. Hal plans to double-cross Falstaff in a robbery, but when he is alone he says he will soon amend his life. The Percys (Hotspur, his father Northumberland and uncle Worcester) arrive at court, and after an angry exchange with the king begin to plot a rising against him.

Falstaff robs the travellers as planned, but is then robbed himself by the prince. Back in his stronghold in the north, Hotspur discovers that he does not have as much support as he had thought, but decides to press on, ignoring his wife Lady Percy's pleas to be informed of his plans. The king's son, meanwhile, amuses himself in Falstaff's tavern base by letting him embroider his description of the robbery before showing him that he and Poins know the truth. Aware that he must return to the court, he and Falstaff act out his meeting with the king, with each playing both characters. Hal, in the persona of his father, vows to banish Falstaff.

The conspirators meet with Mortimer, who has now joined forces with the man who defeated him, Owen Glendower, and married his daughter. They divide England and Wales between them, but there are arguments between them over this. The prince returns to court, and is chided by his father for neglecting his duties. Hal vows to confront Hotspur and show he is his equal in combat. By now it is clear that war is on the way. Hal secures a commission for Falstaff.

Things go badly for the Percys, as both Northumberland and Glendower send word that they cannot reach them in time. Hotspur resolves to fight on, but Worcester is less hopeful. Falstaff and Hal progress toward Shrewsbury, where they will meet the Percy forces. While they are waiting, Hotspur and the others debate whether to attack immediately or wait to build up their forces. They clash with the king's messenger, but appoint another meeting the next day.

The king meets with the Percys, and offers them peace. Worcester turns him down, as he does not trust him. Hal offers single combat to Hotspur to try and avoid bloodshed. Worcester does not tell Hotspur of the king's offer, and the battle begins. Henry sends his followers into battle disguised as himself as a way of distracting his enemies. One of his main advisers, Sir Walter Blunt, is killed by Hotspur's ally, Douglas, who then attacks Henry. Hal saves the king and defeats Hotspur in single combat. Falstaff, fighting Douglas, feigns death, but rises again claiming he has killed Hotspur. Worcester is captured and ordered to be executed, and the king's forces prepare for more battles in the north and Wales.

ACT I

SCENE 1   King Henry IV's plans for a crusade are disrupted by news of disturbances on the Welsh borders. News also comes that Hotspur, victor at the battle of Holmedon, refuses to give up his prisoners to the king

King Henry IV tells his son, Prince John of Lancaster, and other nobles that though the country is still recovering from its internal wars, he proposes to go on a crusade to regain the Holy Land from Islam. He asks the Earl of Westmorland for news of the preparations. These have been disrupted, Westmorland tells him, by news that Mortimer, fighting on the Welsh borders against Owen Glendower, has been captured. In addition, other news arrived that the English noble Harry Percy (Hotspur) had fought against Archibald at Holmedon, but that the outcome was unsure. Work on the crusade was consequently suspended. Henry has had more recent news from Sir Walter Blunt, however: Hotspur has won the battle, and taken some notable prisoners. The king's delight at the victory is soured, however, by Westmorland's comment that it is a victory for a prince to boast of, for it reminds him of the misbehaviour of his other son, Prince Henry (Hal). Hotspur is what a prince should be, so much so that Henry wishes he could exchange him for his own son. Hotspur has, however, not passed on his prisoners for the king to ransom. According to Westmorland, Hotspur's uncle, Thomas Percy Earl of Worcester, is behind this. Hotspur is sent for to account for himself before the Council.

> The opening scene begins with Henry's **imagery** of an exhausted nation, shaken, pale, and out of breath through war. The order of things has been disturbed; the land itself has drunk the blood of its own offspring, and the fact that Englishmen faced each other in opposed armies, shows, in the same way that there being too many meteors in the sky does, that nature itself has been disrupted. This vivid description of the consequences of war contrasts strongly with later more positive characterisations of it as the testing-ground of personal honour.

> To unite the nation after this ordeal, Henry has proposed another war, but this time abroad, and for (it is implied) a just cause. His

y

description of its religious justification, ending with an image of the crucified Christ, is interrupted by the practical matter of Glendower's military successes (and, indeed, the crusade is never seriously reconsidered in either of the *Henry IV* plays). The original concept of war as barbarous is reiterated, this time through the description of the atrocities committed on English corpses by Welsh women (one of the play's several associations of femininity with the threatening and unsettling). In contrast, Hotspur's battle, success in which displays his honour, is described in more abstract terms: 'sad and bloody hour' (line 56), 'heat/ And pride of their contention' (line 60). It produces prisoners (imagined as prizes) rather than corpses. The dual vision of war articulated here is one of the play's themes, recurring most strongly in Falstaff's words and actions at Shrewsbury field.

Westmorland's reply to the king's triumphant rhetorical question deflates Henry, and introduces another of the play's major themes, the contrast between the two young Henrys – Harry Percy and Prince Hal. Shakespeare altered historical fact to produce this contrast, for Hotspur was born in 1364, and Hal in 1387. Hotspur's achievements, moments before a source of joy, now upset the king, as they are in pointed contrast to those of his own son, who lacks Hotspur's virtues, particularly his honour. Hotspur's denial of prisoners, seemingly a defiance of the king, is attributed to the influence of his uncle; both Hal and Hotspur, it later emerges, have to cope with their potentially (in Hotspur's case, actually) ruinous reliance upon older men.

2 **frighted peace to pant** for startled peace to catch its breath

3 **short-winded accents of new broils** out-of-breath words of new battles

4 **strands afar remote** the Holy Land. Henry's intention to lead a crusade is made clear at 19

7 **trenching** wounding, ploughing

12 **intestine** internal

13 **close** close fighting

21 **impressèd** conscripted

23 **mother's womb** England

29 **bootless** useless

30 **Therefor** for this

31 **cousin** kinsman

35 **limits of the charge** specifics of the task given

36 **all athwart** all across (our intentions)

41 **rude** uncivilised

52 **Holy-rood day** Holy cross day, 14 September

55 **Holmedon** Humbleton in Northumbria

58 **shape of likelihood** the likely outcome

69 **Balked** piled up. A balk is the ridge between two ploughed furrows

82 **minion** favourite

84 **riot** revelling

86 **night-tripping** night-walking

90 **coz** cousin

91 **prisoners** Hotspur was entitled to keep all his prisoners except Mordake

97 **prune** preen

97–8 **bristle up the crest of youth** prepare to attack, continuing the image of Hotspur as a trained bird of prey

106 **out of anger can be utterèd** should be uttered in anger

SCENE 2   **Falstaff tries to persuade Hal to join in with a robbery. Poins proposes he and Hal play a trick on Falstaff and rob him once he has got the money**

Falstaff asks Hal the time of day, and is mockingly rebuked for acting out of character. Falstaff, in the first of several references to the time when Hal will be king, proposes new and respectable names for those who live by night, and then asks him if he will hang thieves when he comes to power. Hal proposes that Falstaff will, because he will make him hangman. Falstaff retorts that it suits his melancholy mood, and goes on to tell the prince that he was recently scolded in the street about him by one of the king's councillors. He blames Hal for leading him astray, and vows to reform, but when Hal suggests a robbery tomorrow he enthusiastically welcomes the idea, claiming that thieving is his trade. Poins enters and tells them the plan to rob pilgrims in Kent early the next morning. Hal demurs, despite Falstaff's attempts to persuade him. Poins asks for privacy to persuade the prince, and Falstaff leaves. Once they are alone, Poins proposes they disguise themselves, avoid the robbery itself, and then rob Falstaff and the others in order to hear the story Falstaff will tell. Hal agrees, and on Poins's departure, speaks a **soliloquy**, in which he claims that he is merely experimenting with this life, the better to make an impact when he shows his true colours to the world.

> This scene is in sharp contrast, both in tone and form, to its predecessor. It is predominantly in prose rather than verse, and is full of wit and high spirits. The scene begins with an extended verbal contest between Falstaff and the prince, during which both demonstrate their ingenuity. Falstaff's simple enquiry about the time prompts the prince's proof that Falstaff should not be interested in the time of day (and is thus being 'superfluous'), and that such an interest is a sign of his 'fat-wittedness'. His true interests, Hal argues, are food, drink, and sex rather than minutes, days, clocks, dials and the sun. Part of Hal's ingenuity is his ability to develop a **conceit**, and this metaphorical ingenuity is one of the distinguishing features of his relationship with Falstaff. Falstaff, in his turn, uses a fencing term to acknowledge that the prince has made a good opening, before parrying by developing his point in another direction – he agrees that he is concerned with night rather than the time of day, as he is a purse-taker.
>
> Once this aspect of their relationship is established, another is developed: that Hal will one day be king. Falstaff, after casually making a multiple pun on the prince's grace (or lack of it), asks that thieves should be renamed in order to point up this special relationship with the night, demonstrating his own verbal facility in his list of possible names: 'squires of the night's body' (line 24), 'Diana's foresters' (line 25), 'gentlemen of the shade' (line 26), 'minions of the moon' (line 26), 'men of good government' (line 27). Hal then acknowledges the quality of Falstaff's response, before going on to show that it is appropriate in other ways. Thieves' fortunes ebb and flow, just as the sea does under the moon's influence. Their purses ebb and flow, and so do their fortunes from below the scaffold to the top of the gallows.
>
> Falstaff's subsequent change of subject is challenged by the prince's equally irrelevant talk of buff jerkins, and though Hal's rhetorical question 'what a pox have I to do with my Hostess?' (lines 47–8)

allows Falstaff to begin a series of double entendres shared between them, the fat knight returns to the question of hanging thieves in mid sentence, interrupting another pun (here/heir apparent) to do so. There are two futures, it seems: one, a topsy-turvy and playful one, in which Falstaff and his companions will fulfil their every wish, and the other where business, including execution of thieves, carries on as usual. Hal parries the question, by proposing to appoint Falstaff hangman, punning that he will at least obtain his suits that way. The topic changes to the fat knight's melancholy, with the pair producing between them seven 'unsavoury similes' for it.

Falstaff in his melancholy takes upon himself the persona of the virtuous religious man tempted into attachment to the world (vanity). He returns to this self-characterisation throughout the play, particularly in connection with the question of recognising faults and reforming. Falstaff's vow to reform here, however, is immediately shown to be shallow: Hal mockingly points out he has quickly reformed from praying to purse-taking; Falstaff equally mockingly claims it as his vocation.

Just as he equivocated over hanging, Hal dithers over the robbery, agreeing and then disengaging himself. He eventually decides to rob a thief, which is a less serious transgression than Falstaff's robbery-for-real; furthermore, it is for a joke rather than the money itself. Hal's reluctance to compromise his position as heir apparent with either serious law-breaking or promises for the future is then consolidated in his solo words at the scene's end. Speaking in verse rather than prose (to signify his high social status), he explains to the audience (who may be the 'you' of the **soliloquy**'s first line) that he will indeed reform. Though he distances himself from the Hal we have seen so far, he uses figurative language as he has throughout the scene, developing a comparison between himself and the sun (a traditional image of royalty that recurs throughout the play). His basic point is that virtue is seen to its best advantage when it is compared with ('set off' by) fault. Comparison – between Hal and Hotspur, Hal and Henry IV, Hal and Falstaff, Henry IV and Falstaff – is one of the principal elements of the play's structure. Critics have usually taken the prince at his word here, rather than seeing him as

y

guiltily trying to justify his bad behaviour to a disapproving audience. Certainly Hal's soliloquy here introduces an element of **dramatic irony** into his subsequent appearances, particularly those with Falstaff, who despite the seeming affection between them will eventually be 'thrown off', along with Hal's loose behaviour – though not in this play.

3   **sack** sweet wine

4-5   **thou hast forgotten … truly know** you have forgotten the right way to ask for what you really want

9   **leaping-houses** brothels

10   **taffeta** material associated with prostitutes

13   **come near me** nearly hit me (a fencing term)

14   **seven stars** the Pleiades

15   **'by Phoebus … so fair'** perhaps a line from a song

16   **wag** joker

17   **grace** a multiple pun – 'grace' is both an appropriate address for royalty, and divine favour. Falstaff extends the pun by saying that Hal does not have enough grace (the prayer before meals) even for the small meal of egg and butter

22   **roundly** straightforwardly

23   **Marry** a mild oath, 'Mary' (Christ's mother)

24   **body** retinue

25   **Diana** goddess of hunting and the moon

29   **steal** rob and sneak about

41-2   **honey of Hybla, my old lad of the castle** the town of Hybla was famous for its honey. Hal is perhaps punning on Falstaff's 'original' name of 'Oldcastle' (see Background: Theatrical and Literary Background)

42   **buff jerkin** leather jacket

43   **of durance** long-lasting

45   **quiddities** quibbles

49   **called her to a reckoning** asked for the bill, punningly implying Hal has had sex with her

59-60   **And resolution … Father Antic the law** and courage so frustrated by the ridiculous old law

63   **brave** fine

68-9   **it jumps with my humour** agrees with my temperament

71   **obtaining of suits**   the granting of requests for advancement

73   **'Sblood**   abbreviation of the oath 'God's blood'

74   **gib cat**   tomcat

      lugged   tormented, baited. Bear-baiting was a popular Elizabethan spectator sport

77   **hare**   eating hare was believed to induce melancholy

78   **Moorditch**   a ditch in London, near the madhouse Bedlam

80   **comparative**   comparison-making

82   **vanity**   pride; here used in the sense of a mistaken focus upon the ephemeral

82-3   **commodity**   supply

84   **rated**   scolded

88-9   **for wisdom ... regards it**   a composite quotation from the Bible (Proverbs 1:20, 24)

90   **iteration**   repeating Scripture

96   **an**   if

100   **Zounds**   abbreviation of (and pronounced to rhyme with) the oath 'God's wounds'

      make one   join in

101   **baffle me**   strip me of my knighthood

104   **vocation**   literally, 'calling'; trade. Falstaff alludes to the Bible (1 Corinthians 7:20)

106-7   **set a match**   organised a robbery

117-18   **breaker of proverbs**   someone who goes against the common sense contained in proverbs

121   **cozening**   cheating

124   **Gad's Hill**   place near Rochester in Kent notorious for robberies

126   **vizards**   masks

128   **bespoke**   requested

134   **chops**   fat-face

139   **royal**   coin worth ten shillings

      stand for   make the effort for

154   **poor abuses of the time want countenance**   the problems of the time need the attention of the powerful

156-7   **latter spring! ... All-hallown summer**   youthful old age; fine weather around All Saint's Day (1 November)

173   **appointment**   accessories

177   **buckram**   rough cloth

177 **nonce** occasion

183 **forswear arms** give up my ambitions to be noble

186 **wards** defensive postures (a fencing term)

188 **reproof** disproof; also scolding

194 **unyoked humour** undisciplined mood

196 **contagious** bearing disease

205 **rare accidents** exceptional and unforeseen events

210 **sullen** dull

213 **foil** something against which something else looks better

214-15 **I'll so offend … I will** I will behave like this to become skilled in it, but then I will make up for lost time when nobody expects it

SCENE 3   **The king complains to Hotspur about the prisoners and Mortimer's treachery. Left alone, Hotspur, his father and his uncle decide to rebel against Henry IV**

The king, meeting with the Percy family, assures the Earl of Worcester that his patience is at an end, and brushes aside Worcester's protests. Worcester having been dismissed, the Earl of Northumberland claims that the prisoners were not as strongly refused as has been said. Hotspur explains that the mistake arose because of his irritation with the messenger, whose comments and manner were inappropriate to a battlefield. Henry retorts that whatever the manner of Hotspur's denial, he still will not give up his prisoners until Mortimer – whom the king considers a traitor – is ransomed. Hotspur denies Mortimer is a traitor, but the king contradicts him and leaves after once more demanding the prisoners. Worcester re-enters, and an enraged Hotspur explains to him what has occurred. Worcester points out that Henry has reason to fear Mortimer as he is the heir named by the king Henry has deposed, Richard II. The three then discuss their past support for Henry (now referred to by his surname Bolingbroke, rather than by his royal title), and their lack of reward. Worcester proposes a dangerous plan; before he can explain it, Hotspur excitedly indicates he is ready for any project, however dangerous, as long as it is honourable. Worcester and Northumberland try to calm Hotspur down, but it is not until they offer to leave that he composes himself to listen to Worcester's plan: to gather together Henry's enemies in Scotland, England and Wales and rebel against him.

Y

No sooner has Hal promised to reform than the focus once more shifts to political conflict. The king is again in council, as in the first scene, but this time he faces a direct challenge from those who have helped him to the throne. Though the king takes a strong line with Worcester, dismisses Blunt's attempt to smooth over the conflict, and altogether behaves 'majestically', he does not impress Percy or his older relatives. Percy is given a long speech early in the scene which serves both to justify his behaviour and to add depth to his characterisation. His description of the battle angrily juxtaposes his own tiredness from the fight with the manner of the servant demanding prisoners, who is by contrast presented as feminine (his concern with smells, his use of effeminate language, his recipes for bruises). This messenger is blind to the real sufferings of the living around him; the only concern he shows is his stylised complaint for the wounding of the earth by digging for gunpowder. Percy here, by showing his irritation with these characteristics, defines himself as the opposite – plain speaking, focused, and masculine. It is good enough for Blunt, but not for the king, who directly turns to Mortimer's alliance with Glendower, accusing this traitor of treason, and refusing to ransom him as Percy requests.

Percy's defence of Mortimer reveals his strong attachment to the honour to be gained in battle, and begins the play's serious exploration of the limits and potential of honour. For Hotspur, Mortimer cannot be a traitor because he fought, in true knightly style, hand to hand with Glendower. Such straightforward masculinity, signified by Mortimer's wounds, is incompatible with political calculation ('bare and rotten policy'). Henry, the politician, doesn't see it this way, however; for him, the duel is simply a story.

Whether it is because Henry is not impressed by these images of honour, or as a result of his blunt ultimatum on his departure, Hotspur drops his courtly submissiveness, and impulsively answers back. Northumberland immediately spots that his temper has got the better of him. Worcester, returning, reveals that he is something of a politician himself with his bald statement that he's not surprised that Henry refused to ransom Mortimer. Henry's assumption of legitimate authority is revealed as shaky; Mortimer is a rival claimant to the throne. Hotspur again is given a long speech to reflect on the implications of this, and of his own family's implication in Henry's coming to power. His concern with shame, and what the world thinks of his uncle and father, should not be understood as a modern concern with public opinion: rather, it is of a piece with his overriding passion for honour. Dishonourable behaviour is rewarded with public disapproval (which in turn is recorded for posterity in the chronicles). But there is practical politics involved too. The king has turned against them. Hotspur urges them to try to regain their honour.

What this means in practice is rebellion. But no sooner has Worcester begun by saying that what will follow will be dangerous than Hotspur excitedly welcomes danger as the testing ground of honour. As Hotspur's rhetoric becomes more exaggerated, his uncle and father become more frustrated with him. Hotspur moves from imagining ways of gaining honour to ways of crossing the king and prince Hal, until Northumberland challenges his masculinity by saying that he talks like a woman (that is, emotionally and self-centredly). Hotspur implicitly accepts the rebuke, as he then tries to justify his excessive emotion by calling to mind Bolingbroke's smooth talk before he became king. Hotspur's own excessive language then gives way to Worcester's simple statement of his plan, and the scene ends in a relatively low key.

This scene gives a glimpse of the realities of the exercise of power. Henry may behave and talk like a king, but he cannot rely upon the dignity of his position to inspire obedience. In fact, Henry's position itself is called into question as an alternative explanation for his hostility to the Percys is suggested. Hostpur's concern for honour as the crucial factor in life is shown in depth, but his uncle Worcester shows that while honour is invaluable in battle, something less confrontational is appropriate in practical politics. Hotspur's deference to his elders in these matters shows that he himself is aware of this.

6 **condition** natural tendency
10 **house** extended family
13 **portly** imposing

16 **peremptory** obstinate

18 **frontier** a moody servant is as unwelcome as a troublesome frontier to a monarch

26 **misprision** misunderstanding

33 **new reaped** just shaved

34 **harvest-home** the end of harvest

35 **milliner** hatmaker – hats were often perfumed

37 **pouncet-box** snuffbox

   ever and anon every minute

45 **holiday and lady terms** not everyday or masculine terms

49 **popinjay** parrot

55 **God save the mark!** God protect me!

57 **parmacity** from spermaceti, a substance derived from whales

59 **saltpetre** an ingredient in the making of gunpowder

64 **unjointed** disjointed

67 **Come current** be accepted as

77 **proviso** condition

86 **indent** enter into agreement

99 **confound** spend

100 **changing hardiment** exchanging tough blows

112 **belie** misrepresent

126 **make a hazard of** risk

127 **choler** anger. One of the four basic components of personality, according to the theory of humours

135 **cankered Bolingbroke** rotten Bolingbroke. Referring to the king by his surname rather than his title is disrespectful

144 **of blood** in line to the throne

161 **subornation** persuasion

163 **second** secondary

171 **gage** engage

196 **start** frighten from cover

206 **half-faced** two-faced

207 **apprehends a world of figures** understands many rhetorical devices

237 **pismires** ants

247 **candy deal** sugared amount

278 head army

ACT II

SCENE 1   Early in the morning on the day of the robbery, Gadshill
explains the thieving plan to the Chamberlain

Two carriers complain about the lack of service at the inn: how the quality
of care for the horses has declined since the death of Robin Ostler and that
the fleas that have bitten them both. When Gadshill, rather than the ostler,
eventually responds to their calls, they are rude to him, and leave. Gadshill
then tells the Chamberlain who is to be robbed, and that some eminent
people, including Falstaff, are to be the robbers.

The atmosphere again changes abruptly, as from the council chamber
the action moves to an inn before sunrise. The two carriers taking
food to London rapidly agree that the establishment is not the best –
the horses' food is low quality, there are fleas everywhere and they are
not even provided with a chamberpot and consequently have to use
the chimney. They mistrust Gadshill – they will not lend him a
lantern, and won't even tell him the time or when they intend to
arrive in London. After they have left it transpires that Gadshill is
indeed untrustworthy, as the Chamberlain informs him of likely
victims to rob. The association of thieving with hanging, made in the
play's second scene, is here continued, as Gadshill tells the Chamberlain
that if he hangs, Falstaff will hang too. Indeed, Gadshill works with
no common thieves, for he boasts that the thieves are themselves
socially eminent, preying on the community when they should be
praying for it. The status of thieving itself is changed by their
involvement, as, if necessary, they could 'make all whole' (lines 73–4).

- *1* **by the day** in the morning
- *2* **Charles's Wain** the Plough or Great Bear
- *4* **Anon** in a minute
- *5-7* **put a few ... out of all cess** stuff some wool into the saddle, because the poor
  horse has an excessively bruised backbone
- *8* **dank** damp
- *9* **bots** stomach worms
- *16* **tench** the markings on this fish were thought to result from stings or bites

21 **jordan** chamberpot

22 **chamber-lye** urine

loach fish thought to breed parasites

49 **'At hand ...'** here I am; a contemporary catchphrase

55 **franklin** rich freeholder

62–3 **Saint Nicholas' clerks** highwaymen. Saint Nicholas is the patron saint of travellers

70 **Troyans** hearty companions

74–5 **foot-landrakers, ... long-staff sixpenny strikers** thieves travelling on foot, thieves who would knock you down with a staff for sixpence

75–6 **mad mustachio purple-hued maltworms** bewhiskered, purple-faced heavy drinkers

77 **Burgomasters** chief magistrates

81 **commonwealth** community

87–8 **receipt of fern-seed** fern-seed was thought to be visible once a year on Midsummer's Night. If prepared using a special recipe, it was thought to confer invisibility

96 *homo* Latin for 'man'

SCENE 2   **Falstaff robs the travellers, then the prince and Poins rob him**

Poins hides Falstaff's horse and then hides himself. Falstaff looks for his horse, but cannot find it. Gadshill turns up with Bardolph and Peto, and the four of them rob the travellers. As they share out the money, the prince and Poins, in turn, set upon them and frighten them off. Hal and Poins are left triumphant with the spoils.

This short prose scene opens with a practical joke on Falstaff, who, once he is alone, speaks a **soliloquy**. This solo speech is very different from the prince's at the end of Act I Scene 2, however. Falstaff, whilst complaining about the trick, ruefully ponders his affection for Poins, concluding that only witchcraft or a love potion can explain it. There is no calculation about it, as there appears to be with Hal. Hal's re-entry, and his request that Falstaff lie down to listen for travellers, is met with a self-mocking jest about needing levers to get back up again and a short-tempered promise to have ballads sung about the prince to horrible tunes. While robbing, Falstaff keeps up a running commentary insulting the victims. This scene offers several opportunities for physical **comedy** – Falstaff's difficulties in moving without his horse, his behaviour during the first robbery and the comic fright of the second all have potential. Though a robbery has still taken place, the overall mood is light-hearted, and the scene ends with the prince and Poins laughing at the success of their trick.

2 **gummed velvet** velvet treated to produce a glossy finish this way wore out (or 'fretted') more quickly than otherwise

12 **square** measuring instrument

13 **break my wind** begin to wheeze; fart

36 **colt** trick

43 **peach** inform on you

75 **dole** fate

83 **caterpillars** parasites

87 **gorbellied** potbellied

88 **chuffs** contemptuous term

90 **grandjurors** socially eminent men (another reference to them being fat)

93 **argument** conversational topic

98 **equity stirring** justice alive

107 **lards** drips sweat onto, as lard melts onto meat

SCENE 3   **Hotspur, though he has less support from others than he expected, sets off for the wars, refusing to tell his wife what his project is**

The scene opens with Hotspur reading out a letter from someone refusing to join in the rebellion. He comments mockingly on the reasons given, and recapitulates the present state of the rebels' plot. Worried that the king will find out about the plot from the letter-writer, he resolves to leave immediately. Lady Percy enters, and complains that he has not taken her into his confidence, despite his bad dreams and odd behaviour. Percy evades her questions by changing the subject and finally by directly refusing to tell her.

This short scene is built around two long speeches. Percy's opening monologue (a kind of dialogue with the absent letter-writer) both confirms the progress of the rebels' plot and, through his increasing irritation, reinforces for the audience the character's impetuousness.

Lady Percy's long speech addressed to her husband immediately upon her entry presents, however, another Hotspur: one who is nervous, pensive and melancholy while awake, and prone to dreams of battle while asleep. Hotspur's response to her questioning is to ignore it, calling for his servant and questioning him about horses. Like Richard III faced with Margaret's curse in Shakespeare's *Richard III*, he interrupts her questions with facetious remarks, before telling her that the world has no place for love. He refuses either to tell his wife where he is going or that he loves her, and the scene ends with her reluctantly bowing to his decisions.

Hotspur's persona when reading the letter, even though he is alone, is his public one – confident, short-tempered, argumentative. But Lady Percy reveals another side of him, and of the honour code he has already celebrated so hyperbolically. Hotspur, for whom honour is all, seemingly cannot admit his own fears to himself, or share them with his wife. Nor can he tell her what his plans are, despite her having a shrewd idea of her own that he will support a rival claimant to Henry's throne. Rebellion is a man's business (and the letter-writer keeping clear of it merely 'skimmed milk'). Love, for him, is feminine – playing with dolls, jousting, but only with lips. Against his ingeniously slippery use of language to avoid Lady Percy's accusations, the scene contrasts her directness in asking whether he loves her or not. This reverses one of the standard gendered assumptions about language – that men are simple and direct, and women talk too much. In doing so, some of the contradictions in the honour code surface.

9 **take** catch
13 **unsorted** unsuitable
14 **for the counterpoise of** to equal
33 **go to buffets** hit myself
43 **stomach** appetite
54 **palisadoes** fence made of spikes
55 **basilisks** large cannon
    culverin small cannon
64 **hest** command
75 **Esperance!** hope! (the Percy family motto)

81 **deal of spleen** amount of irritability

88 **paraquito** parrot

95 **mammets** dolls

    to tilt with lips joust with lips; kiss

97 **pass them current** use them for currency. A pun on 'crown' (head, but also a coin)

    God's me! God save me!

120 **force** necessity

SCENE 4   **Hal and Poins arrive back at the tavern and amuse themselves by tormenting Francis, the drawer. When Falstaff enters, they listen to his imaginative account of the events at Gad's Hill before revealing that they know the truth. Hal and Falstaff each impersonate King Henry to prepare Hal for his meeting with his father. Hal then diverts the officers of the law who are searching for Falstaff in connection with the robbery**

Hal begins the scene by describing to Poins his familiarity with the tavern world, and sets up a practical joke on Francis. The prince engages him in conversation whilst Poins keeps calling for him from another room. Hal gradually begins to deliberately confuse Francis until, not knowing whether to try and answer the prince or go to Poins, he 'stands amazed, not knowing which way to go' (stage direction). Hal mocks Hotspur, and then Falstaff and the others return. Falstaff, in a bad mood, enters cursing cowards and moaning about the state the world has reached. He accuses Poins and Hal directly of cowardice, and calls for drink. Once it has arrived he tells his story of the robbery, exaggerating the numbers and fighting involved, and produces his sword (so damaged that it looks like a saw) as evidence. The numbers increase as the story proceeds, until Falstaff is claiming he fought with over fifty. The same thing happens with his account of himself being robbed; at the beginning there are two robbers, but by the end there are fourteen. Hal and Poins, listening to the story growing, comment sardonically on each fresh invention. Finally, Hal points out that Falstaff has contradicted himself in saying the robbers wore green and that it was too dark to see. Falstaff refuses to explain 'upon compulsion' (line 232), whereupon Hal plainly tells what happened.

Falstaff then claims that he knew all along what was happening, and that he subdued his natural courage so as not to hurt the prince. He suggests they enjoy themselves by improvising a play, but before they can start he is called to the door, where a courtier is asking for Hal. While he is offstage, Bardolph and Peto explain how Falstaff faked the evidence of the fight. Falstaff enters again with the news that Hal must return to the court to help deal with the Percy rising. They decide to practise Hal's return so that he can cope with his father's scolding. Falstaff begins as Henry and warns Hal about the company he keeps, saying that it will stick to him as pitch does, though he excepts himself from the general condemnation. They change places, Falstaff becoming Hal and the prince becoming his father. Hal's impersonation of the king is much more critical of Falstaff, who defends himself and ends by pleading with 'the king' not to banish him from the prince's company. Hal responds, 'I do, I will' (line 466), but the tension is immediately broken by knocking on the door. Falstaff hides, and Hal covers for him with the sheriff, who is seeking the Gad's Hill robbers. Falstaff has fallen asleep, and the prince finds a bill in his pocket for meat and sack. The scene ends with Hal saying he will go back to the court and put Falstaff in charge of a section of the army.

> This tavern scene provides the play's only extended presentation of the non-courtly world, Falstaff's natural habitat, and its culture. Such a culture is no more assimilable to the world of King Henry's rule than to Hotspur's community of 'honour'. Its main features in this scene are good humour and laughter, invention, playfulness, and solidarity, and its king is Falstaff, who dominates the action for a large part of this scene. His tall story to Hal ascends ever brighter heavens of invention as he exaggerates for effect, but his real vindication is not his ability to excuse his being robbed, but his split-second improvisation in response to Hal's exposure of him as a fraud. Like Hal, Falstaff is skilled with words, but this skill is in the service of amusement and play.

> But this world is already under threat from the outside, because Falstaff, its principal inhabitant, is pursued by the law and must go to the wars. It is also threatened from the inside, in the person of Hal.

> In Hal's first **soliloquy** (Act I Scene 2) he claims to repudiate the

'idleness' and 'unyoked humour' of the tavern world. The scene's opening demonstrates that his own participation in the world he claims only to be studying, includes using his verbal dexterity – already demonstrated in conversation with Falstaff – to bamboozle Francis the drawer. Francis is, however, no Falstaff, and is reduced to mute confusion. Though Hal claims in his first speech to Poins to be 'sworn brother to a leash of drawers' (lines 5–6) and friends with 'all the good lads' (lines 13–14) of the area, his practical joke is hardly evidence of this. The laughter here is more cruel than celebratory (which is not to say that the scene isn't funny in performance). But Hal explains to Poins that his self-aware playfulness differentiates him from the unintentionally funny single-mindedness of Hotspur, for whom killing 'six or seven dozen of Scots at a breakfast' (lines 101–2) is a 'quiet life' (line 103). In contrast, Hal's exposure of Falstaff's lies is less aggressive, functioning more as a challenge to Falstaff's ability to improvise a new explanation for his actions than a repudiation of the man himself: 'What trick, what device, what starting-hole canst thou now find out?' (lines 257–8).

Hal's impersonation of his own father, however, indicates his ability to understand and reproduce the courtly perspective on the world he currently inhabits. This extends to a condemnation of Falstaff, and a resolution to banish him from his own company. When speaking as his father, Hal's characterisation of Falstaff contrasts sharply with Falstaff's own, more comic, self-presentation, as having 'virtue in his looks'. In Hal's speech, all Falstaff's virtues are insignificant – his goodness, cunning and craft are put to trivial uses, and are counter-balanced by his villainy 'in all things' (villainy at this time still also connoted low social status, a 'villein' being a medieval peasant). Falstaff understands the subtext of Hal's speech, and pleads not to be banished. Hal/Henry says 'I do, I will' (line 466). It seems at this moment that Hal, through his words in the kingly role he was born to play, is throwing off his loose behaviour, as he promised in Act 1 Scene 2.

But the action is interrupted by the sheriff's knock, and in the brief period before his entry Hal quickly slips back into his laddish self. When Falstaff continues to insist he is not what he seems, comparing himself to Hal's own doubleness in this regard ('Never call a true piece of gold a counterfeit. Thou art essentially made without seeming so', lines 477–8), the prince facetiously remarks that Falstaff is a 'natural' coward, just as he seems to be. He then goes on to assume yet another role – 'a true face, and good conscience' (lines 486–7) – for the sheriff, to whom he speaks in verse. It is in this serious vein that he resolves to go to court, and it is this seriousness, rooted in Hal's role as prince, that threatens the Eastcheap world. During this scene, the contrast between Hal and Falstaff is strongly drawn. Though both are witty and delight in language's possibilities, and both adopt roles at the drop of a hat, Falstaff is always playing to (and with) the same audience. In contrast, Hal is seen as both tavern trickster (with Francis and the Gad's Hill story) and authority figure (with the sheriff and, implicitly, when he replies as 'king' to Falstaff).

4   **loggerheads** blockheads
5   **hogsheads** casks
7   **leash of drawers** three tapsters
11   **Corinthian** party animal
23   **underskinker** under wine-waiter
26   **bastard** sweet wine
36   **Pomgarnet** pomegranate
46   **indenture** apprenticeship agreement
109 **Rivo!** drinking cry
113 **nether-stocks** stockings
116 **Titan** sun
120 **lime** added to wine to make it sparkle
125 **shotten** thin
132 **dagger of lath** stage dagger, used by Vice characters (see line *441*)
163–4 *ecce signum* Latin, 'look at the evidence'
186 **peppered** killed
211 **hose** stockings
224 **tallow-catch** vessel to catch fat from cooking
233 **strappado** form of torture which jerked arms from their sockets
240 **starveling** thin person
     elf-skin small amount of skin
241 **neat's-tongue** ox tongue

241 **pizzle** penis

stock-fish dried cod

242 **tailor's-yard** yardstick

243 **standing tuck** rapier standing on its end

258 **starting-hole** bolt-hole

264 **Hercules** mythical Greek warrior famed for his strength

273 **extempore** improvised: literally, 'from this time' in Latin

287 **gravity** old age

303 **beslubber** make sticky

306 **devices** devisings

313 **exhalations** the earth was thought to sometimes 'exhale' (breathe out) meteors

316 **livers** the producer of the passions

318 **halter** noose; Hal puns on 'choler/ collar'

320 **bombast** material used for padding; metaphorically, high-flown language

329 **Amamon** a devil

bastinado beating on the soles of the feet

331 **Welsh hook** pike

350 **blue-caps** Scots

366 **chid** scolded

371 **state** throne

373 **joint-stool** stool produced by a joiner, therefore professionally made

380 **Cambyses' vein** in the style of the play *Cambyses* (1569), which was considered old-fashioned by the time of *Henry IV Part I*

386 **tristful** sorrowful

387 **tears do stop the floodgates** her eyes are blocked up (stopped) with tears

390-1 **tickle-brain** strong drink

401 **micher** truant

414 **by'r lady** abbreviation of by Our Lady, a mild oath

418 **peremptorily** decisively

426 **rabbit-sucker** baby rabbit

poulter's hare hare bought from a shop

436 **tun** large barrel, punning also on 'ton' weight

438 **bolting-hutch** sifting bin, thus full of residue as Falstaff is full of 'beastliness'

439 **dropsies** dropsy is retention of fluid and consequent swelling of the body

bombard large wine container

441 **reverend Vice** the Vice character, as his name implies, led characters into evil ways, often aided by his virtuous ('reverend') appearance

441 **grey Iniquity** a Vice's name, also referred to in Shakespeare's *Richard III*

442 **Vanity** another personification of vice, this time pride

451 **Pharao's lean kine** the story is in Genesis 41

481 **major** the main premise of the argument

485 **arras** curtain

502 **withal** additionally

511 **Paul's** St Paul's cathedral

524 *ob.* (Latin) halfpenny

526 **deal** amount

530 **charge** company

531 **twelve score** two hundred and forty

ACT III

SCENE 1   **Hotspur and Worcester meet with Mortimer and Glendower in Wales to plan their campaign and divide the country between them. The business concluded, Mortimer's wife and Lady Percy meet with their husbands**

The meeting begins in discord, as Hotspur mocks Glendower's claims that his birth was accompanied with supernatural signs, and that he himself is learned in magic. The three sides proceed to divide England and Wales up, with Glendower taking Wales and the land west of the river Severn, Mortimer taking England south and east of the Severn and the Trent, and Hotspur the northern remnant. After they have arranged their military affairs, Hotspur complains that he has the smallest share, and proposes to change the course of the Trent. Glendower objects, and the two clash again, before both backing down. On Glendower's exit, Mortimer scolds Hotspur for his mockery. Hotspur again criticises Glendower's tedious obsession with magic, and is reminded by Worcester that this quick temperedness does not become a noble. Hotspur quietens, and Glendower returns with Lady Percy and his daughter, Mortimer's wife, who speaks to her husband in Welsh, which he cannot understand. She then sings a song in Welsh. Hotspur tries to persuade Lady Percy to sing, but she refuses. Hotspur leaves, and the scene concludes with Glendower announcing that the document embodying the agreement has now been drawn up.

The scene's opening, with the king's opponents in confident mood, quickly establishes how serious their threat now is, and refocuses the play on the political world beyond the tavern walls. The former opponents, Mortimer and Glendower, are now related by marriage, and the talk is of the king's fears. As earlier, Henry is not given his royal title, being referred to here as 'Lancaster'. This united front, however, very quickly appears to have its own problems. Hotspur angers Glendower by insisting that the 'supernatural' signs accompanying the latter's birth would have happened anyway, even if the only event was a cat having kittens, and by bluntly stating that he does not fear him. Hotspur redescribes the earthquake Glendower mentions, personifying the earth as suffering from trapped wind. Glendower insists, adding that he is naturally learned in magic. Hotspur's response, typical of his linguistic strategy in this scene, is deflationary: 'no man speaks better Welsh' (line 47) – that is, to an English audience, better gobbledygook. When Glendower claims to be able to call spirits, Hotspur retorts that anyone can *call* spirits. Revealingly, Hotspur's criticism of Glendower makes it plain he considers him a liar, and that Hotspur's insistence on telling the truth (and thereby shaming the devil) also leads him to mistrust self-conscious rhetoric. When Glendower tells of how he has sent Bolingbroke three times 'bootless' home, Hotspur mocks the word, and in doing so mocks Glendower's rhetoric.

The scene then rather abruptly shifts from this conflict, in which Hotspur and Glendower play out the roles of plain speaker versus rhetorician already occupied by Hal and Falstaff respectively in the previous scene, to the division of Henry's kingdom. England is to be, figuratively, dismembered, and its river to be dammed and diverted to suit Hotspur and Worcester. This proposed alteration of the natural world for political purposes sparks off another disagreement between Glendower and Hotspur, showing both the extent to which the land itself will be affected should Henry be defeated, and the likelihood of further conflict in the future (a theme Shakespeare revisited a decade later in the division of the kingdom in *King Lear*). The theme of speech again recurs, this time with Glendower reminding Hotspur that he can speak – and sing – good court

English (and, implicitly, that Hotspur cannot). Hotspur responds by making his earlier point more explicitly, this time with a disparaging reference to 'mincing poetry'.

The masculine world of public affairs is again contrasted with the domestic feminine world, as Glendower comments that his daughter will 'run mad' on Mortimer's departure. This is not the first mention of women's emotions (and the 'femininity' of affection in general), however; Hotspur's proposal to redraw the boundaries by changing the course of the Trent directly follows Glendower's earlier remark, which implicitly addressed the Percys, that 'there will be a world of water shed/ Upon the parting of your wives and you' (lines 90–1). Just as he had earlier when Lady Percy confronted him on his leaving in Act II Scene 3, Hotspur changes the subject. In fact, what he objects to in Glendower, it turns out once the Welsh leader has left, is in some part his 'feminine' garrulity. He compares him to a 'railing wife', though his other examples – a smoky room and a tired horse – are not gender-specific, turning instead on their capacity to irritate. Hotspur's irritability, Worcester reminds him bluntly, is a 'fault' in the wrong context. What is 'greatness, courage, blood' in one setting is 'harsh rage,/ Defect of manners, want of government,/ Pride, haughtiness, opinion, and disdain' (lines 178-9) in another, and indeed has the capacity to negate all other virtues. It is not the first time the point has been made.

These virtues are primarily public and, broadly, political. Mortimer ironically comments that the 'deadly spite' which angers *him* is his lack of a common language with his wife. This line functions both to show how far Mortimer is from Hotspur's plain English hotheadedness, and how far Hotspur himself is from the everyday domestic world. On the introduction of the women, the scene's tone shifts toward the domestic and personal. Hotspur says little for a while, and much of what he does say is privately addressed to Lady Percy. The Mortimers and Glendower take centre stage, and play out a love scene which parallels Lady Percy's earlier one with Hotspur. The central difference, of course, is that Glendower and his daughter speak in Welsh, and so the focus is primarily upon Mortimer's responses, which combine an insistence that he will leave with a recognition of his own emotions. As with Hotspur, he is conscious of the requirements of public decorum: 'but for shame' he would reply to his wife's 'parley' with his own tears. Mortimer and his wife do not banter as Hotspur and Lady Percy do, and the effect, perhaps particularly when the action stops dead while 'the lady sings a Welsh song', is to remind an audience of the non-public world, and the way in which war impinges upon this world too.

The mood is broken, however, by Hotspur, who loses his temper with his wife after she refuses to sing. The principal cause, however, appears to be the inappropriateness of Lady Percy's oath 'in good sooth'. She swears, Hotspur says, like the wife of a 'comfit-maker' (a sweet-maker). In other words, her daintiness reflects badly upon him, as if he were somebody (implicitly) unmanly. The respectable 'Sunday citizens', out in their Sunday best 'velvet guards', may speak so, but she is not of their social class. She should swear 'like a lady as thou art,/ A good mouth-filling oath' (III.1.247–8). Perhaps unsurprisingly, Lady Percy refuses again to sing, and her husband leaves without her.

- 2 **induction** beginning
- 12 **front** face
- 13 **cressets** small metal baskets filled with material on fire
- 28 **enlargement** release
- 29 **beldam** grandmother
- 31 **distemperature** disorder
- 41 **clipped** held
- 46 **hold me pace** keep up with me
- 60 **made head** raised an army
- 63 **Bootless** unsuccessful
- 76 **indentures tripartite** agreement in triplicate
- 92 **moiety** share
- 94 **comes me cranking** twists back at me
- 96 **cantle** segment
- 108 **charge** cost
- 125 **canstick** candlestick
- 143 **the moldwarp and the ant** the mole and the ant; a prophecy, supposedly by Merlin, about the political future of the island

147 **couching** lying down

ramping rearing up; Hotspur here parodies heraldic language

157 **cates** delicacies

161–2 **profited/ In strange concealments** proficient in hidden arts

183 **Beguiling** depriving

199 **feeling disputation** a heartfelt argument

204 **division** musical variation

225 **humorous** changeable

230 **brach** bitch

242 **comfit-maker** sweet-maker

245 **sarcenet** flimsy; sarcenet is a silky material

246 **Finsbury** area in north London

249 **protest of pepper-gingerbread** mildly spicy oath

250 **velvet-guards** clothes trimmed with velvet

253 **turn tailor** tailors had a reputation for singing at work

253–4 **redbreast teacher** teacher of caged birds to sing

SCENE 2   **Hal meets his father, who rebukes him for his irresponsible life. The prince promises to behave more appropriately. When the king praises Hotspur, Hal retorts that he will soon have his rival's reputation, and the scene ends with preparations for war**

Once he is alone with his son, the king pulls no punches in his criticism, suggesting that his son is a divinely sent punishment for his unspecified 'mistreadings'. Hal answers evasively that it will be easier to answer these charges than many others, and after a brief mention of the unreliability of public opinion offers his 'true submission'. Henry expands on his misgivings, which are only partly about Hal's character. His main worry is what he sees as the prince's political mistake in making himself too visible to and with commoners. The king refers back to the contrast between his own 'seldom seen' state and that of the king he deposed, Richard II, who, like Hal, 'mingled his royalty with capering fools'. Indeed, Henry notes ironically, the only person who does not see enough of the prince is himself. Not only is Hal like Richard II, but there is a new Henry to depose him, in the shape of Hotspur, whose chivalric virtues make him more worthy of the crown than Hal's 'weak succession'. The king is not even sure whether his own son will fight for him. Hal's reply once again claims that he has been misrepresented, and reiterates his determination to redeem himself. The two are reconciled, and Hal is immediately given new military responsibilities as Blunt interrupts.

> Most of this scene is static, as it is composed largely of long monologues during which Henry challenges Hal or Hal defends himself. But action is never far away: at the opening, Henry tells his lords to remain nearby 'for we shall presently have need of you', and the scene ends with Blunt's interruption of the action with news of the meeting at Shrewsbury. In this first meeting in the play between son and father both run true to type. Henry's dissatisfaction with his son and Hal's plan to 'redeem' himself (the word nicely conflating paying back a debt and cancelling past sins) are already familiar to the audience. Not only have both sides' feelings been made clear earlier in the play, but the interview itself has already been played out in parody between Falstaff and Hal in Act II Scene 4. Falstaff's question in that scene, 'Shall the blessed son of heaven prove a micher, and eat blackberries?' (II. 4. 400–1) is a more specific version of Henry's later condemnation of 'Such poor, such bare, such lewd, such mean attempts' (line 13). But whereas the earlier scene primarily revolved around Falstaff's relationship with Hal, this scene has no mention of him by name. Hal's reassumption of his role as heir apparent is here figured not, as earlier, as a betrayal of his father-figure Falstaff, but as the proper expression of his filial loyalty to his actual father. Falstaff may be king in Eastcheap; but for the court, Hotspur is pre-eminent in his 'never dying honour'. Hal must imitate Hotspur as well as shun Falstaff.

> Royalty, the king's opening words make clear, is partly a matter of living up to the example set by ancestors. Hal's deficiencies are made the more obvious because his younger brother has taken his place in Council. But just as important is Hal's failure to win the 'hearts' of the nobles of the realm. Henry's coming to the throne, he reveals, depended upon this relationship, which Hal must get right. Kings rule in practice through the consent of the ruled, and a crucial component of this is 'sun-like majesty'. Hal has made himself too familiar to the people, 'every beardless vain comparative' (line 66). This might

seem no bad thing, but the king shows, by developing a metaphor of oversweetness, how 'a little/ More than a little is by much too much' (lines 72–3). Instead of imitating his father, Hal resembles the man he usurped, and is thus a poor son as well as a poor prince.

Henry's account, of both Richard's fall and his own success, seems oddly disjunctive with the events of this play (and, for that matter, of the presentation of Richard's supplanting in Shakespeare's earlier *Richard II*). Henry, after all, does not have any relationship with 'the people'. But the king's problem is the same as he predicts Hal's will be; those he wishes to obey him – the greater nobles – are not in awe of him. They remember him not behaving as a king, not because he was dissolute like his son, but because he was merely one of their own. The king's account of his own virtues and Richard's deficiencies also helps to prepare the ground for a second extended comparison, this time between his son and Harry Percy. 'Opinion' fuels the Hotspur rising; he has 'no right, nor colour like to right' (line 100) in his cause, but is able to fill fields with his supporters, nonetheless. Privately, as the audience has seen, Hotspur is less imposing; but his reputation and achievement in the public sphere is huge. Hotspur's reputation, Henry notes, has been gained by the quality of those he has challenged and defeated. Hal takes the point, proposing to seek honour Hotspur's way, in combat.

12 **inordinate** inappropriate
15 **grafted to** physically joined to
17 **hold their level** keep their place
25 **pickthanks** tale tellers
30 **wing** course
36 **thy time** your maturity
61 **bavin** wood used for kindling (hence, soon consumed by the fire)
62 **carded** scratched
66 **stand the push** put up with the crowding
67 **comparative** Falstaff calls Hal 'comparative' at 1.2.80
69 **Enfeoffed** gave himself completely to
71 **surfeited** had too much
77 **blunted with community** tired of too much contact
83 **cloudy** frowning

109 **majority** eminence
112 **Mars** Roman god of war
120 **Capitulate** make agreements
125 **start of spleen** fit of anger
132 **redeem** make good
136 **favours** armour decorations
147 **factor** agent
148 **engross up** collect
172 **advertisement** news

SCENE 3   **Falstaff is challenged to pay the hostess what he has
borrowed. The prince arrives bringing news of the war and
Falstaff's new status as officer**

The scene begins with Falstaff in contemplative mood with Bardolph,
considering whether he should repent his life as he is getting old. Bardolph
responds that such pensiveness is sure to shorten his life, and Falstaff perks
up, reflecting that he has not been so bad. Bardolph's gibe about his weight
leads him into an extended retort about the latter's red nose. The hostess
enters to try and claim Falstaff's debt to her. He attempts to distract her,
but she persists until the prince enters with Peto. Mistress Quickly appeals
to Hal, but Falstaff counterappeals that his pocket has been picked in her
house. The hostess tells the prince that Falstaff has been claiming that the
prince owes him money and will beat him if he does not get it. Hal defies
Falstaff, and scolds him for his lies about the contents of his pockets.
Falstaff realises that the prince has picked his pocket, and apologises to the
hostess. Once she has gone, Hal tells Falstaff the news that he has paid
back the money from the robbery, been reconciled to his father, and
secured Falstaff a charge of foot. Falstaff complains he would rather have
had horsemen, but Hal's attention has shifted to the practical arrangements
for their leaving.

> The whole scene is governed by a dynamic in which Falstaff, initially
> in complete command of his situation despite his low spirits, is
> forced to deal firstly with the hostess's insistence that he repay her,
> and then with not only the more formidable adversary of Hal, but
> also the realisation that he himself must go to the wars. It opens, in
> contrast to the urgency with which the preceding scene ends, with

Falstaff's low-key musings upon his health, and his complaint that 'villainous company' has led him astray. He appears at the point of repenting his life, and is as restrained as he will be anywhere in the play. But whereas in the previous scene Hal's promise to reform himself is taken seriously, Falstaff's resolution lasts only seconds. Bardolph's proverbial remark that sadness and short life go together ('care's an enemy to life', as a character in *Twelfth Night* put it) is quickly picked up by Falstaff, however, as a cue to cheer up. He remarks that he has been 'virtuous enough', and provides a catalogue of his virtues – whilst undercutting each as he mentions them. Bardolph's attempt to pun on Falstaff's fatness produces another stinging reference to his own red nose, this time likened to a lantern in a ship. Re-energised, and now in full flow, the fat knight continues to improvise on themes Bardolph unwittingly suggests, producing paradoxical 'proofs' that keeping company with him stimulates pious thoughts (the red nose reminds him of hellfire) and that it enables economies on torches (because Bardolph's nose lights the way). From beginning the scene using his rhetorical gifts to anatomise himself, Falstaff has now shifted into a more characteristic mood, that of exercising his wit on his immediate surroundings.

Another victim then presents herself, as the hostess enters with the news that there is no news of Falstaff's pocket being picked. Whilst the hostess walks into traps Falstaff sets for her, responding to his scornful 'Go to, you are a woman, go!' with the indignant denial 'Who I? No, I defy thee!' (lines 60–1), she is not simply filling in time as Bardolph was. She wants money from Falstaff, and presses him repeatedly for repayment. Falstaff is unable to put her off, and even his managing to turn the conversation back to Bardolph's nose does not get him off the hook. Prince Hal's sceptical attitude toward Falstaff's boasts has rubbed off on the hostess, who tells Falstaff that the prince assured her that the family heirloom seal ring, supposedly lost in the pickpocketing, is actually only copper.

The prince's entry with Peto 'marching' gives the hostess the chance to appeal to him, and push Falstaff more onto the defensive. Falstaff responds by continuing to insult her, and Hal briefly joins in, feeding the line 'Why an otter?'. He soon assumes his more familiar role of antagonist to Falstaff, however, putting him on the spot about his lies to the hostess. Falstaff attempts to wriggle away, claiming he has been misunderstood, but Hal confronts him directly: 'darest thou be as good as thy word now?' (lines 141–2). He goes further, and attacks Falstaff himself, much more directly than he has so far, ending by asking him if he is not ashamed at his duplicity. Falstaff drops back into his 'preacher' persona, pointing out that if the flesh is frail, he is bound to be frailer than most because of his size. He has not missed, however, the implication that Hal picked his pocket.

Once the hostess has left, Falstaff becomes more personal, asking Hal for 'the news at court'. Hal's changed attitude is further shown by his refusal to play the games he had in his first scene with Falstaff. Each statement of his, about the robbery, his relationship with his father, and his procuring Falstaff a charge of foot, produce a joking response from the fat knight. Where earlier in the play this might have been Hal's cue to produce his own joke in reply, the prince here does not register Falstaff's interventions at all, simply moving on to the next item in his list. His distance from Eastcheap is finally signalled by his switch into verse as he gives orders to Bardolph, Peto, and finally Falstaff. His language with his former comrades indicates his assumption of his royal status, and his final couplet before leaving shows how completely he is now focused on the coming confrontation: 'The land is burning, Percy stands on high,/ And either we or they must lower lie' (lines 200–1). Falstaff is given his own couplet to end the scene on a more downbeat note. He mocks both Hal's language and his new persona, before signalling his reluctance to leave: 'Rare words! Brave world! Hostess, my breakfast, come!/ O, I could wish this tavern were my drum' (lines 202–3). The language indicates that the scene has, in a sense, two endings, with neither Hal's nor Falstaff's perspectives dominant. Leaving Eastcheap means different things for different characters.

2 **bate** shrink

4 **apple-john** apple whose skin shrivels but which remains edible for a long time

7 **An** if

8 **peppercorn** worth very little and very small

brewer's horse known for being old and tired

20 **compass** order

30 ***memento mori*** Latin, 'reminder of death' (to keep the Christian's thoughts on the next world)

31 **Dives** the story is in Luke 16

39 ***ignis fatuus*** Latin, 'will o' the wisp' (literally 'fool's fire')

42 **links** torches

51 **dame Partlet** Falstaff implies the hostess resembles a hen in her fussiness

68 **Dowlas** cheap linen

69 **bolters** cloths used for sieving

70 **holland** fine linen

71 **ell** 45 inches

78 **denier** one-tenth of a penny

79 **younker** young man; the prodigal son was the youngest son

89 **Newgate fashion** two by two like prisoners

112 **drawn fox** fox drawn into the open and thus relying on cunning to deceive its hunters

155 **embossed** swollen

158 **make thee long-winded** give you energy

182 **with unwashed hands** without wasting time on niceties

119 **furniture** equipment

ACT IV

SCENE 1   **In Hotspur's and Worcester's camp, news arrives that Northumberland and his forces cannot join them. Worcester fears that this absence will affect morale. Hotspur prefers to see it as increasing the heroism of the enterprise, and welcomes the news that Hal is on the way to meet them. Further news that Glendower too will not come in time arrives**

The scene begins with Hotspur and Douglas exchanging compliments. Letters arrive from Hotspur's father indicating that he is sick, and has been bedridden for four days. Worcester quickly indicates how crucial this absence is likely to be. Northumberland's letter, which Hotspur summarises for the others, indicates that his father's potential followers have not responded to his agents, and that as he himself is too ill to appeal

y

to them, no forces have been raised either. Despite this, the letter advises that the die is cast, and that the Percys must meet the king in battle. Worcester responds that this is a poor option too, but Percy, after initially agreeing with him, takes the opposite point of view. Northumberland's absence means that they are not gambling all their resources at once. Douglas agrees that this knowledge means they can be more bold in battle.

Worcester interrupts this morale-boosting with a flat contradiction. Their attempt should *not* be divided, not because of the military forces lacking, but because the Earl's absence will 'breed a kind of question in our cause' (line 68). Hotspur disagrees, reiterating that their success so far with only a portion of their forces shows that 'men must think/.../ with his help/ We shall o'erturn' (lines 79–82) the kingdom. Vernon enters bearing more messages that the king and Prince Hal are coming. Hotspur takes the chance to joke about Hal, but the messenger's reply praises Hal's appearance and his skilful movements in his armour. Hotspur is much more bothered by this praise than by the earlier news, cutting the messenger off. Seizing on the praise of Hal he compares them to sacrificial offerings 'in their trim', and looks forward to meeting the prince in combat. Vernon continues, and his news that Glendower also will not arrive daunts both Worcester and, for the first time, Douglas. Hotspur ends with an attempt to rouse his fellows, and both he and Douglas end the scene vowing they are not afraid to die.

> The scene opens *in medias res*, to indicate the speed at which events are now moving, and, as the scene in Wales did, opens with an amicable exchange between Hotspur and one of his allies. As with Act III Scene 1, however, this harmonious opening is soon disrupted, but not before Douglas has called Hotspur 'the king of honour' (line 10). The phrase nicely points up the way in which honour offers an alternative set of loyalties and priorities to those of the nation – Hotspur is the king of one, and Henry the king of the other. Hotspur's honour in this scene is primarily shown as fearlessness. It is more honourable, he assures Worcester, to fight against bad odds, for it lends 'A larger dare to our great enterprise' (line 78). Such an honourable dare, in turn, will rally the morale of the Percy side.

> Though not as skilled in language as Hal, Hotspur understands also that one of his functions is to rally his side, and this scene shows him

consciously using language to do so, firstly in his attempt to interpret Northumberland's absence positively, and more obviously after the description of Hal in armour. He uses the very positivity of Vernon's description against Hal and, seizing on the way sacrifices are similarly well-presented, redescribes them as offerings to Mars, the god of war. As in the scene preceding it, Act IV Scene 1 ends with couplets, Hotspur having two and Douglas having the last word with a rhyme of his own. Unlike the previous scene, Douglas's final speech does not undercut his predecessor. Rather it indicates that Douglas, who earlier had taken the news about Glendower badly, is ready again for battle, and that the Percy powers appear to have got over the various unwelcome messages in the scene.

Despite this strong closure, however, Worcester's words are not necessarily forgotten. Hotspur convinces himself and Douglas, but he does not convince Worcester, and perhaps not audience or reader either. There is a limit to Hotspur's ability to positively interpret matters. His brusque silencing of Vernon's praise of Hal ('No more, no more!', line 111) is a moment perhaps when his own ability to build himself up is disabled by Vernon's own eloquence. His own rhetoric in reply to Vernon is markedly more concrete, and harsher in subject matter than it has been before.

7 **soothers** flatterers

9 **approve** test

12 **beard** come face to face with

18 **justling** jostling

36 **advertisement** advice

37 **conjunction** alliance

47 **cast** of the dice

    main stake

48 **nice** delicate

51 **list** limit

54 **reversion** inheritance

59 **maidenhead** early stage

61 **hair** detail

71 **loop** loophole

96 **daffed** tossed aside

98 **estridges** ostriches

104 **beaver** helmet

105 **cuishes** thigh armour

106 **Mercury** Roman messenger of the gods

109 **Pegasus** winged horse from Greek mythology

134 **Doomsday** judgement at the end of the world

SCENE *2*   **Near Coventry, Falstaff comments on the progress of his force so far. Hal arrives and tells him to hurry to Shrewsbury for the forthcoming battle**

Falstaff and Bardolph have a brief exchange about provisioning, with Bardolph complaining that he has not yet been reimbursed for his outgoings. Once he has left, Falstaff admits that he has 'misused the king's press damnably' (lines 12–13), by choosing recruits who are able to buy themselves out of service. To take their places he has assembled a 'dishonourable-ragged' band, who are so dirty that he dare not march through the main town in the area (Coventry) with them. Hal enters with Westmorland, and confirms Falstaff's opinion. His men are indeed 'pitiful rascals' (line 62). Falstaff protests that this is none of his doing, and all three exit on the way to Shrewsbury.

> The centre of this short scene is Falstaff's **soliloquy** on his recruits. He has made money from them, for he picked those who could buy their way out – good householders, yeomen's sons and the like. The result is that his men are a motley crew. This is a typically Falstaffian tour de force, playing variations on a theme ('discarded unjust serving-men, younger sons to younger brothers, revolted tapsters, and ostlers trade-fallen ...', lines 26–8) and showing his ingenuity in description. This comic exuberance is later radically qualified by his shockingly dismissive remark to Westmorland that they are 'good enough to toss, food for powder, food for powder, they'll fill a pit as well as better' (lines 63–4). This throwaway remark obviously gives an insight into Falstaff's character – he is not an honourable man. But he cannot be. Honour in the play is shown as exclusively the preserve of nobles, usually in the idealised context of single combat between equals. Such options are not available to the common

soldiers, who as 'food for powder' (cannon fodder) will die in battle before they get near their enemies (as indeed happens).

The scene functions not only to undercut the idea of war as primarily the venue for single combat, but to qualify the previous scene's information about the king's men. In that scene Hotspur and his fellows do not consider that the king's army may be as undermined as their own, and so it ends with a heroic resolve to fight on against unfavourable odds. It seems that the outcome of the battle is decided, and it will indeed be doomsday for the Percys. But Falstaff's description of his rascals makes it clear that not everyone in the king's army is as formidable as Hal. It also reminds us that more than one main character will be risked during the battle. Falstaff himself is under threat, and with no possibility of honour, what he will make of the battle (and what the battle will make of him) is also foregrounded. His final couplet reminds an audience that, though he may not be looking forward to battle, he has other virtues – a dull fighter, but a keen guest.

After the prince's brusqueness in his last encounter with Falstaff, he speaks to him more affectionately here, even greeting him in the old manner with a variety of names, and even develops one of his jokes ('unless you call three fingers in the ribs bare ...', lines 71–2). He has also reverted to prose, even though another noble is present. Indeed, Westmorland too speaks in prose. The effect is a striking contrast with the highblown verse rhetoric of the previous scene, implying that the king's forces are approaching the battle in a more low-key fashion at this point. That the last words are Falstaff's distinctly unheroic couplet confirms this.

6   **makes** brings the total up to
12   **soused gurnet** small pickled fish
     press conscription
16   **contracted** engaged to be married
16–17 **asked twice on the banns** close to marriage
17   **commodity** amount
19   **caliver** musket
24–5 **Lazarus in the painted cloth** the parable of Lazarus and Dives is in Luke 16

33 **prodigals** reckless youths

34 **draff** swill

39 **gyves** fetters

46 **on every hedge** left out to dry

47 **quilt** because Falstaff is well padded

63-4 **food for powder** cannon fodder

71-2 **three fingers in the ribs** three fingers' worth of fat between ribs and skin

SCENE 3   **Hotspur and his allies discuss whether to attack the king's forces straight away. Blunt brings an offer of parley from the king. Hotspur defies Blunt, reminding him of Henry's weak claim to the throne, but puts off the final reply until the following day**

The Percy forces are divided amongst themselves over whether to attack tonight or wait for supplies. They discuss the state of the king's forces and their own. Blunt interrupts them, and is greeted courteously by Hotspur. The king, through Blunt, promises to redress their grievances and pardon them if they submit. Hotspur's reply is to relate Henry's progress to the throne at such length that Blunt dismissively interrupts him, whereupon Hotspur names their grievances – the refusal to ransom Mortimer, dismissal of his father from the court, and others. When he has finished, however, Hotspur requests more time to consider his final answer.

As with Hotspur's last scene, this begins *in medias res*. The Percy side is split between Hotspur and Douglas, who favour an immediate battle because the king's forces will soon be strengthened, and Vernon and Worcester, who counsel delay because their own forces are not yet strong enough. The division threatens to become personal, as Douglas accuses Vernon of cowardice. Vernon's reply to this 'slander' is to distinguish between caution and cowardice: 'If well-respected honour bid me on,/ I hold as little counsel with weak fear/ As you, my lord, or any Scot that this day lives' (lines 10–12). Cowardice is failing to act when honour demands it, but Vernon denies that honour is at stake at the moment.

Hotspur's greeting to Blunt gives some idea of the honourable approach to conflict. Whilst regretting Blunt's opposition, he praises him. Even those who do not 'love' Blunt recognise his reputation. They 'Envy your great deservings and good name' (line 35). Blunt, however, owes his loyalty not to the honour code but to the nation, and therefore does not return Percy's compliments. His equivalent to Hotspur's compliment is to say that he is 'out of limit and true rule' (line 39). Henry's offer of pardon, and his enquiry about the grievances leading to the rising, for the first time shows him adopting a less confrontational approach. Hotspur's response, however, indicates that he does not consider Henry to be in a position to offer pardon. He delivers the fullest description in the play of Henry's coming to power, and shows just why his family refuses to be described as rebels: 'My father, and my uncle, and myself/ Did give him that same royalty he wears' (lines 54–5). He has seen Henry's 'seeming brow of justice' before, when he usurped the throne from Richard II, and so is unlikely to be impressed by his offers now. His opening words ('well we know the King/ Knows at what time to promise, when to pay', line 52–3) must be interpreted in the light of his later list of Henry's broken promises, including the oath to Northumberland that he only sought his inheritance. Despite the seeming finality of the description of the king's title to the throne as 'too indirect for long continuance' (line 105), the scene's ending, in which Hotspur plays for time, introduces the possibility that he has listened to Worcester's and Vernon's words, and will try to postpone the confrontation until another day.

26 **journey-bated** tired from their journey

33 **determination** resolution

40 **anointed** the monarch is anointed with oil upon coronation as a sign of God's favour

62 **sue** claim

68 **cap and knee** bending the knee with cap in hand; a sign of abasement

92 **in the neck of that tasked** immediately after taxed

96 **forfeited** unclaimed

98 **intelligence** secret information

99 **Rated** scolded

SCENE 4 One of Hotspur's allies, the Archbishop of York, sums up
the perilous state of the anti-Henry forces

The Archbishop of York, who at the end of Act I Scene 3 had been named
by Worcester as a likely supporter of the Percy faction, here sends letters in
an attempt to raise resistance against the king, who now knows of his
opposition to him. He is not reassured by Sir Michael's confidence in the
military strength of the Percy side.

> This short scene is theatrically necessary to indicate the time passing
> between the first and second meetings of the two sides. It summarises
> the state of both, and adds the information that Glendower has not
> arrived because he is 'o'er-ruled by prophecies' (line 18), an element
> of his character that Hotspur has already irritably remarked upon
> (III.1.142–9). The Archbishop, whether or not he has heard of the
> king's offer of pardon, behaves as though it is not likely, which adds
> tension to the encounter to come.

5 **import** mean

7 **tenor** mood

10 **bide the touch** endure the test

ACT V

SCENE 1 King Henry meets with Worcester and Vernon, with Hal
and Falstaff present, to offer peace. Worcester reminds the
king of his actions since coming to power. Henry dismisses
the accusations. Hal offers single combat against Hotspur.
At the end of the scene Falstaff asks Hal to protect him
during the battle, and muses upon honour

After a brief exchange on the weather between the king and Hal, the two
sides meet. The king asks whether Worcester will be obedient once more.
Worcester's reply protests his desire for peace, and that he has not sought
this confrontation. On Henry's scornful reply, Worcester elaborates,
covering much of the same ground as Hotspur had in Act IV Scene 3.
Henry has turned his 'looks of favour' away from the Percys, even though
they helped him gain the crown. He reminds him of his oath, sworn at

Doncaster, that he would not seek further than to regain his inheritance, and recounts the combination of luck, circumstance, help from others and weather that led him to the throne. Henry is to blame for the rising, through his own oath-breaking and threatening behaviour.

Henry's response is that, though this might sound persuasive, it is the kind of thing that rebels *would* say. There is clearly no common ground on which the king and Worcester can negotiate. Hal, who has only spoken to shut Falstaff up, then intervenes to offer Hotspur single combat to avoid both armies having to fight. Henry confirms that this is acceptable to him, and reiterates his offer of pardon to Worcester, who leaves to convey the offer to Hotspur. Once Worcester has gone, Hal says that he does not think the offer will be accepted, and his father exhorts his followers to be ready for battle. Left alone with Hal, Falstaff asks him to 'bestride' him if he falls in battle, and looks forward to when the battle is done. Once Hal has left, Falstaff speaks a **soliloquy** on honour, in the form of a catechism (a series of questions and answers normally used as a religious mnemonic).

The scene opens in reflective mood, with the king comparing the sun's redness to blood. Once he has met Worcester, however, his tone changes. He describes Worcester as a planet out of orbit, looking like a meteor in the sky and signifying no good. Worcester replies to this in plain language, but develops some metaphors of his own in his long speech narrating Henry's coming to power. His speech adds little factual detail to Hotspur's, but two such long speeches, so close together, serve to show both the grounds of the Percy rising, and to cast doubt upon both Henry's claim to the throne and his personality. Henry's metaphor for Worcester's 'disobedience' places it in the realm of cosmically significant events. Worcester, however, describes Henry dismissively as a cuckoo, unjustly displacing others. He concludes by reminding Henry that his own treatment of the Percys during the play, and his faithlessness during the time preceding his usurpation of the throne, have brought matters to this pass. Henry responds with some dismissive language of his own, characterising Percy sympathisers as simpletons and 'moody beggars'.

Behind this verbal clash, as elsewhere in the play, is the tension between loyalty to the honour code and loyalty to the nation. Up to this point, the king's side has not shown any inclination to claim they are honourable rather than legitimate. But now Hal steps forward, in best chivalric style, to challenge Hotspur to single combat. His adoption of the honour code also shows in his praise of Hotspur:

> I do not think a braver gentleman,
> More active-valiant or more valiant-young,
> More daring or more bold, is now alive
> To grace this latter age with noble deeds. (V.1.89–92)

Despite Hal's offer, and Henry's protestation that 'we love our people well' and offer of pardon, once Worcester has left Hal advises his father not to expect submission from the Percys, precisely because of the bravery he has just praised in Hotspur: 'The Douglas and the Hotspur both together/ Are confident against the world in arms' (lines 116–7).

The relationship between Hal and Falstaff is once more strained when they are alone, though earlier Hal had used the affectionate term 'chewet' in quietening Falstaff. Falstaff, as he has several times earlier, speaks directly and is met with a joke. Only a 'Colossus' can bestride Falstaff. Similarly, Falstaff's 'I would 'twere bed-time, Hal, and all well' (line 25) is met with a cold proverbial retort ('thou owest God a death') and an exit.

Once he is left alone Falstaff develops his catechism on honour, turning his wit toward a critique of the honour code. Honour cannot cure the wounds received in gaining it. It is just a word. Honour in death cannot be perceived by the dead. But honour is not secure for the living, because 'Detraction will not suffer it' (lines 38–9) – that is, honour, as public recognition of certain virtues, is vulnerable to public opinion changing. Honour, Falstaff concludes, is a 'mere scutcheon': no use to the living, and Falstaff means to live, as the death he owes is 'not due yet'. Again, the scene's structure enables a complex perspective upon its actions. Even though Hal reaches an important stage in his quest for honour during it through offering single combat to Hotspur, the values that he has chosen to embrace are counterpoised both by Henry's and Worcester's more sophisticated political manoeuvrings and by Falstaff, who gets a last word to further qualify the incipient heroism the scene displays.

3   **distemperature**   uncharacteristic appearance

24   **entertain**   occupy

29   **chewet**   chatterbox

36   **posted**   rode quickly, exchanging horses as they tired

50   **wanton**   ungoverned

57   **gripe**   grip

74   **face**   cover

77   **rub the elbow**   express delight, as rubbing hands today does

88   **set off his head**   put aside

111   **wait on us**   are at our service

112   **office**   duty

123   **Colossus**   giant statue of Helios the sun-god at Rhodes, one of the seven wonders of the ancient world

129-30   **pricks me on**   spurs me on

140   **scutcheon**   tomb memorial bearing coat of arms

SCENE 2   **Worcester and Vernon keep back the king's offer from Hotspur, reasoning that they will be dealt with more harshly than the younger Percy should they surrender. Douglas defies the king, and Vernon tells Hotspur of Hal's challenge. They prepare for battle**

Worcester and Vernon argue over whether Hotspur should know of the king's offer. Worcester is firmly against the idea, first reasoning that the king will never be reconciled to them, and will always regard them as he would a constrained but still wild animal. Furthermore, whatever they do will be liable to misinterpretation. Hotspur may be forgiven, as he is young and impetuous, but they will not. Once Hotspur enters, Worcester simply tells him that battle is imminent. Once Douglas has returned their defiance to the king, Worcester tells him of Hal's offer of single combat. Hotspur initially wonders whether it is a joke at his expense, but Vernon then, as he has in Act IV Scene I, praises Hal extravagantly, and stresses he is now 'like a prince indeed'. Hotspur is sceptical ('Never did I hear/ Of a prince so wild a liberty', lines 70–1), and applies himself instead to preparing for the battle. He refuses to read letters that have newly arrived, and reminds the others that victory will mean 'treading on kings', while death will be in good company. Justice is on his side. He draws his sword, and calls for the trumpets to signal the start of battle.

The scene again uses the division of the Percy camp into the cautious Vernon and Worcester, and the combative Hotspur and Douglas. It begins, once more, *in medias res*, with Worcester replying to what seems to be Vernon's proposal to let Hotspur know of the king's peace terms. Worcester does not trust the king, and uses animal images to indicate their likely status should peace be taken. They will be mistrusted as a fox would, and will simply be animals waiting for slaughter, 'like oxen at a stall' (line 14). It transpires, however, that the 'we' he uses does not refer to all of the Percys. Hotspur's impetuous character – signalled by his nickname – may protect him from reprisals. The older, and more cautious, 'as the spring of all shall pay for all' (line 23). Worcester thus, in an attempt to save himself, will deceive Hotspur. This does not necessarily mean he is deliberately prepared to sacrifice Hotspur for his own ends. He does not trust Henry at all; Hotspur's offences *may* be well forgot, but may not be. Henry's proposal for pardon follows hard on a condemnation of the Percys as rebels.

The discussion between Worcester and Vernon does not consider how Hotspur might take the offer of peace, only the consequences should it be accepted. This may indicate an awareness that even Hotspur, in delaying the previous night, is having second thoughts, but Hotspur's own scornful response to the idea that Worcester might 'beg' mercy of the king makes such an interpretation difficult to maintain. The long speeches given to Hotspur and Worcester show their positions as essentially the same: Henry is untrustworthy, has a poor claim to the throne, has treated his former allies badly and has forced the Percys to rise against him by his high-handed behaviour. The only disagreements between Worcester and Hotspur have been over whether to fight the king now or later. If Worcester and Hotspur are of the same mind, then, the question of whether Hotspur would now accept the kind of promises from the king he so firmly rejected when Blunt offered them in Act IV Scene 3 must be left open.

Vernon's praise of Hal confirms his difference from his father. None of the Percy faction have a good word to say for the king, but Vernon's glowing descriptions of Prince Hal confirm him as conforming to the honour code (one of the essential qualifications for this being praise from your opponents). Ironically, the 'king of honour', Hotspur, does not recognise this impartial praise as evidence that Hal's reformation is to be taken seriously, though as the recognised leader of the Percy forces he has other things on his mind. As befits his image of himself as a plain speaker, he twice denies he has the 'gift of tongues' to make a rousing speech, directing his listeners instead to 'our consciences' and 'what you have to do'. The height of his eloquence is 'Only this -/ Let each man do his best' (lines 91–2).

7 **in** using the excuse of
8 **Supposition** wariness
18 **adopted name of privilege** nickname giving immunity
38 **forswearing** falsely swearing
50 **tasking** challenging
54 **proof** test (hence, the exception that proves – tests – the rule)
55 **duties** due praises
56 **Trimmed up** decorated
61 **cital** reference
74 **courtesy** martial ability; Hotspur is emphasising that he is not a courtier
96 **Esperance! Percy!** the family motto, used also at Act II, Scene 3, line 75

SCENE 3   **Blunt, disguised as Henry IV, is killed by Douglas. Falstaff and Hal briefly meet and argue**

The battle having begun, Douglas challenges Blunt, who he thinks is the king. He has already killed one nobleman, the Lord of Stafford, who claimed to be Henry. He demands that Blunt surrender, and when Blunt refuses, he fights with and kills him. Hotspur, entering, congratulates Douglas, but knows Blunt, and tells Douglas who he is. Douglas vows to keep on until he meets the king, and both exit.

Falstaff enters, and finds Blunt's corpse. He is tired, and those few men of his that survive ('three of my hundred-and-fifty', lines 36–7) are wounded and will have to beg for the rest of their lives. Hal enters, and demands Falstaff's sword. Falstaff claims his exhaustion is from his valiant fighting, and claims to have killed Hotspur. When Hal again asks for his sword, he offers him instead his 'pistol', which turns out to be a bottle of sack. Hal, disgusted, throws the bottle at him and leaves. Falstaff, left alone

                                         Y

again, faces the possibility that he may die in battle, but still prefers life to the death with honour that has met Blunt.

The scene opens with a stage image of chivalrous single combat, but this is ironically undercut by Blunt's deception of Douglas, and the unchivalrous, if politically astute, tactic adopted by the king of using decoys, some of whom have already died in battle. This undermining of the play's heroic image of battle continues in Falstaff's first **soliloquy**. Here his language is more sanguine than in previous scenes. His wit and wordplay are back in evidence; he puns on 'score' and finds two similarities between himself and molten lead. He is equally dismissive of his 'ragamuffins' 'peppered' to death and Blunt: 'there's honour for you!' (lines 32–3).

The new Hal is disgusted with Falstaff's punning and his offering him a bottle of sack, asking 'is it a time to jest and dally now?' (line 55). Once Hal has left, Falstaff, undaunted, continues in the same vein, punning again on Percy's name, and vowing to avoid him. The sight of Blunt's corpse leads him to the vivid death's head image of 'grinning honour', summing up the grotesqueness of claiming any kind of positive outcome for such a death. If he does gain honour himself in battle it will not be because he has sought it, but because he is dead. As long as he lives he will take the dishonourable route of survival. This scene again combines differing elements to enable a complex response. Blunt's corpse is onstage during Falstaff's joking with himself and Hal. Though the scene begins with a single combat, Falstaff again gets the last word.

stage direction **Alarum** loud noise
21 **Semblably** seemingly
25 **coats** coats of arms
30 **shot-free** without paying the bill (score) in a tavern
38 **town's end** town gates
41 **vaunting** boasting
45 **Turk Gregory** combines the common tyrannical figures for Elizabethans of Muslim and Pope
58 **a carbonado** piece of meat to be grilled, kebab-style

SCENE 4   The king's forces regroup, and he fights Douglas. Hal
rescues his father. Hotspur and Hal finally meet, and
Hotspur is killed. While they fight, Falstaff meets Douglas
and feigns death to escape. Hal pays tribute to Hotspur and
Falstaff, after which Falstaff gets up and wounds Hotspur's
corpse. Meeting Hal, Falstaff claims he killed Hotspur, to
the prince's amusement. The battle ends

Henry tries to get Hal, who is wounded, to retreat. Neither he, nor his
younger brother John of Lancaster, do so. Lancaster heads back into battle
with Westmorland, to Hal's admiration. The king is left alone and is
confronted by Douglas, who, though he initially thinks he is another decoy,
admits he does bear himself 'like a king' (line 35). Douglas gains the
advantage when they fight, but Hal returns to rescue his father, and
Douglas flees. Hal's action finally shows his father his reformation is in
earnest. Henry leaves for the battle, and Hal then meets with Hotspur.
Hotspur recognises Hal, and introduces himself. Hal makes clear his
intention to claim Hotspur's honour in combat. While they are fighting,
Falstaff enters and, after commenting for a while, has himself to fight
Douglas. He feigns death, and Douglas leaves.

Hal wounds Hotspur, whose final speech regrets not his death but
losing his 'proud titles'. He speaks his own epitaph, which Hal completes.
Once Hotspur has died, the prince speaks a **eulogy** over the corpse, and
covers its face. He then spots Falstaff, and eulogises him also, though his
language remains relatively formal. Once he has left, Falstaff gets up, and
ingeniously explains how he is not a 'counterfeit': a corpse is more false, as
it is the body of a man with no life. He sees Hotspur's body, and wounds it
to make sure it is dead. Intending to claim the credit for Hotspur's death,
he picks the corpse up, and is met by Hal and Lancaster. He claims he has
killed Hotspur, and improvises a response to Hal's report of seeing him
'Breathless and bleeding on the ground' (line 132). Hal agrees to support
Falstaff's claims, and Falstaff is left alone again, to look forward to his
reward.

This scene is the climax of the play. Each of the four main characters
is involved. Hal rescues his father and defeats Hotspur, thus proving
himself to be both loyal to established power and capable of

achieving honour. The king shows himself to be brave against Douglas. Hotspur loses both his life and his reputation to Hal. Falstaff 'dies' and is resurrected.

For most of the play the king's forces do not claim to be as eminent in honour as the Percys. In this scene, however, the king and his two sons acquit themselves well in battle. The conflict between honour and legitimate royal power, between military glory and loyalty to the nation, is resolved, primarily through Hal's combination of the two. Not only does he defeat Hotspur, but he does so whilst giving him due credit. As he is also loyal to the king, however, his praise is qualified, so that 'great heart' is immediately followed by 'ill-weaved ambition'. His newly tested loyalty is also demonstrated in the way he eulogises Falstaff. He begins, appropriately enough, with a witty reference to the fat knight's size ('could not all this flesh/ Keep in a little life?', lines 101–2) and follows it with the emotional 'I could have better spared a better man' (line 103). But his next line shifts from what he feels to what he will feel, as he states he would miss him, but only if he was in love with vanity. In other words, Hal implies, rather tortuously, that he will not miss Falstaff. Despite this, when he finds out Falstaff is still alive, he seems to slip back into his old role as protector, saying he will lie 'to do thee grace' (line 156). His lack of consistency, and his constant qualification of what he says, indicates the conflicting claims on his affections – political and familial (to his father), honourable (Hotspur) and personal (Falstaff).

Falstaff himself here lives to fight another day, and even ends the scene vowing another one of his reformations, though this time the motivation is not religious so much as social. If he gains the earldom or dukedom he expects as his reward for killing Hotspur he will bear himself 'cleanly as a nobleman should do' (line 164). The dead Hotspur becomes a physical prop in a boastful routine, just as Blunt's corpse was the occasion for his wit earlier. Here Falstaff puts into practice his cynical insights on honour, by planning to manipulate public opinion to make himself seem honourable. But Hal's cheerful response indicates that this is not a serious possibility (it would be difficult to reconcile Hal's determination to take Hotspur's honour with a willingness to pass the credit on to another).

stage direction **excursions** groups of soldiers crossing the stage

21 **maintenance** bearing

24 **Hydra's heads** the Hydra was a many-headed beast which could grow new heads to replace any cut off

33 **assay** test

47 **opinion** reputation

64 **sphere** orbit

87 **Ill-weaved ... shrunk** poorly made cloth shrinks after washing

89 **bound** boundary

95 **favours** cloth decoration for armour

108 **Embowelled** disembowelled as part of preparations for burial

111 **powder** meat was powdered with salt or spices to preserve it

112 **termagant** arrogant character, from supposed Muslim god with these characteristics in medieval plays

128 **fleshed** introduced to flesh

129 **maiden** untested

SCENE 5   **The king condemns the captured Worcester and Vernon to death, and prepares his forces to meet the remaining rebels in the north and west**

The king attacks Worcester's ingratitude, and particularly his failure to deliver the king's offer of 'grace' to the rebels. Worcester stoically refuses to admit he is at fault. Once Worcester and Vernon are condemned to death, Henry asks for news, and is told of Douglas's capture. He grants Douglas to Hal, who in turn tells his brother John of Lancaster to release him without ransom in recognition of his valour. Henry then divides his forces, sending John and Westmorland to the north, while he and Hal head west to confront Glendower. The scene ends with the reflection that the work of putting down the rising is half done.

This final scene opens with Henry's confident moralisation of the situation. His attack on Worcester reminds the audience that the Hal–Hotspur fight of the preceding scene, despite its aptness as the climax to the play, need not have happened. The great chivalric contest, already undercut by Falstaff, is ironically further downplayed. Worcester responds with his own display of virtue, stoic fortitude in the face of what fortune has brought him. The scene's focus on honour is continued with Hal's description Douglas's flight and his ordering John to free the Scot, in implicit contrast to the divisive treatment of prisoners at the play's opening. Despite Falstaff and Worcester, chivalry is still alive, and proper display of virtue is rewarded. Hal's own reassumption of his proper role is signified by his brother respectfully addressing him as 'your grace'. But though chivalry – and Hal – remain intact, the state of Henry's regime remains poised, and the play ends not in triumph but with exhortation toward renewed efforts.

20 **Upon the foot of fear** in panic
29 **crests** helmets
33 **give away** pass on to Douglas
36 **dearest** best
41 **sway** rule

PART THREE

CRITICAL APPROACHES

CHARACTERISATION

There are three elements contributing toward our sense of a character: what they say and do when with others, what they say and do when alone and how others refer to them when they are not present. *Henry IV Part I* is a play deeply concerned with political and other kinds of role-playing, honour and reputation. Is Henry IV as duplicitous as the Percys say he is? Is Hal always as distant from the Eastcheap world as he says he is? Is Hotspur as valiant as he seems? Questions such as these are not always resolvable, but (paradoxically) such ambiguity helps to produce characters that exist in three dimensions.

The play is notable for the variety of its solo speeches. **Soliloquies** in *Henry IV Part I* are not confined to the 'overheard thoughts' model. Hotspur, though alone on stage, enters into a dialogue with the contents of a letter. Falstaff recites a mock-catechism on honour, running through a speech which may or may not be prepared beforehand. Most importantly, the play's solo speeches are not completely committed to the **realist** assumption that the character is always unaware of the audience. As section five notes, Elizabethan drama was **self-reflexive**, reaching out to its audience with a directness realist theatre does not possess. Hal's soliloquy at the end of Act I Scene 2, when he explains his plan of action for the future, is introducing and explaining himself to the audience as well as being explicable in realist terms. The same is even more true of Falstaff's soliloquies, as their comic nature makes them even more likely to work effectively with the audience as addressees rather than overhearers. Falstaff, as befits a character many critics have seen as embodying the vital comic forces within society, could be said to never be truly alone.

FALSTAFF

Though Prince Hal is the play's hero, around whom plots and themes coalesce, Falstaff has historically been its most popular and memorable character (see Critical History and Further Perspectives). This popularity can best be understood by considering Falstaff's character and his function in the play together. His main attribute is his power to amuse himself and others, onstage and off, and he devotes to this end considerable verbal and physical skills. Though he never uses verse, his prose is often complex and makes use of figurative language. An example is his piling up of synonyms for Hal's amusement, just after he has made his first entry:

> Marry then, sweet wag, when thou art King let not us
> that are squires of the night's body be called thieves of
> the day's beauty. Let us be Diana's foresters, gentlemen
> of the shade, minions of the moon. And let men say we
> be men of good government, being governed, as the sea
> is, by our noble and chaste mistress the moon, under
> whose countenance we steal. (I.2.23–9)

Falstaff here puns on knight/night and proposes several inventive new names for thieves. The common element to them all is service. He also attempts to redescribe thieving as service to the moon, and thus prove that theft is actually good order and obedience. Such puns, paradoxes and lists are three typical characteristics of Falstaff's speech when he seeks to amuse. He is also able to use physical **comedy**, most obviously in his mime of the Gads Hill robbery ('I made me no more ado, but took all their seven points in my target, thus!', II.4.196–7). He is physically focused in another way, too: his main desires in life are to eat, drink, sleep, have sex and live without working. He has no ambitions, and few concerns beyond the immediate moment. In his absolute devotion to a version of the good life, Falstaff functions as an embodiment of the irresponsible life. His fatness and his age both add to the overall impression of an enjoyed and irresponsible life. He is not simply, however, a jolly old man; his linguistic ingenuity, and the serious uses he makes of it occasionally, place him closer to another kind of figure.

Falstaff is, in other words, a clown in both the everyday and the Shakespearean senses, and like many of Shakespeare's later clowns he is able to twist language almost any way he wishes, and speak wisdom under the cover of a joke (a good example is his mock catechism on honour at V.1.127–40). His function then in the play is not simply to amuse, but to provide a sceptical and irreverent perspective on the deadly serious business of the main plot. Falstaff's attractiveness is thus not merely a matter of some good jokes and knockabout comedy. He understands, though he does not wish to be part of, the world he mocks, and his commentary on the uselessness of honour adds tension to Hal's pursuit of it, and pathos to Hotspur's eventual loss of it. Many of his lines, especially in his short solo speeches, could equally well be directed at an audience onstage or off.

Falstaff is also to be understood as a character within the plot. He is greedy, deceitful, dodges bills, bullies those less clever than himself, lies, steals and exploits others. His capacity to create laughter of various kinds is thus balanced by some less appealing traits. This mass of deplorable characteristics also serves to qualify the validity of his witty paradoxes. Is Falstaff a coward because he sees through honour, or is his sceptical perspective reducible to a rationalisation of his own comic cowardice? Do we focus on the teller, or the joke, or both?

PRINCE HAL

Hal is the hero of the play in the sense that he is a central character to both subplot and main plot. Furthermore, his progress through the play provides a dynamic portrayal of change, for Hal more than any other character ends the play a different person from the one he was at its start. Hotspur, Henry IV, and Falstaff remain reasonably constant from scene to scene, but Hal spends the first half of the play oscillating between wasting time in Eastcheap and thinking about reforming himself. Unlike Falstaff, however, Hal does reform.

The two key passages in interpreting Hal come early in the play, before he has reconciled himself to his father. The first is at Act I Scene 2, where, after a scene spent joking in Falstaff's company and planning a practical joke, Hal, alone on stage, speaks a soliloquy in a very different persona. As his father will later tell him, controlling public access to royalty is the key to its success. Hal declares he will show his real self infrequently, so that when he does 'throw off' the persona he has adopted it will make a greater impact. From his father's point of view later in the play, Hal has missed the point, which is that royalty should be seldom seen at all.

Many critics have seen this soliloquy as showing that Hal is always detached from the Eastcheap world. It is certainly important to bear this statement of inner purpose in mind when thinking about the play's hero. But it should also be remembered that audience and reader encounter the 'external' Hal as much as, if not more than, the 'real' Hal. How much is the experience of enjoying Hal matching wits with Falstaff changed by the knowledge that Hal had earlier said he despised his companions as 'base contagious clouds' smothering up his beauty from the world (I.2.196–7)? Similarly, the knowledge that Hal, speaking in the person of his father in Act II Scene 4, plans to 'banish' Falstaff does not immediately render the earlier part of the scene, in which he goads Falstaff to ever greater heights of invention, a pathetic demonstration of his secret contempt for the easily manipulable fat knight.

The crucial point in Hal's change from reprobate to model prince could be said to be neither of these passages, but his interview with his father at Act III Scene 2. Here Henry IV not only reproaches his son for neglecting his duty, but advises him on the best way to present himself in the world. It is here that Hal vows to immediately change: 'I shall hereafter, my thrice-gracious lord,/ Be more myself' (III.2.92–3). His sudden reformation is now, for the first time, spoken of as involving Hotspur rather than simply a return to court and repudiation of the tavern world. Henry does not mention Hal's activities in Eastcheap except in the most glancing manner. Hal's ambition to 'command all the good lads in Eastcheap' (II.4.13–14) is superseded by a desire to prove himself to another community, one focused on martial achievement and honour, where Hotspur, not Falstaff, is 'king'.

Once Hal has changed his focus, his attitude to Falstaff changes too. Neither returns to Eastcheap after the mid-point of the play (Act III Scene 3). Up until Hal receives his commission from his father in Act III Scene 2, he shows Falstaff some affection, and energetically joins in, displaying no little skill, with Falstaff's improvisatory wit-games. But once they are settled on the serious business of preparing to meet the Percys, the prince takes a much more judgemental view of Falstaff, refusing to pick up his cues for jokes (III.3.190), scolding him ('Art thou not ashamed?', III.3.160–1), ignoring his request for help during the battle should he need it (V.1.126), and finally, in exasperation, throwing a bottle at him on the battlefield at Shrewsbury (Act V Scene 3).

HOTSPUR

Harry Percy's nickname, as his uncle Worcester notes (V.2.18), sums up his character. He is quick to anger and to speak out, and slow to subside, whether with friend or foe. In this, as in much else, he is at the opposite pole to prince Hal. He has a sense of the ridiculous, and is not afraid to mock. Though he presents himself as a plain-speaking man, he is capable of flights of eloquence. He has already achieved a great deal by the opening of the play, where the king, who we will soon see has no reason to be generous to him, calls him 'the theme of honour's tongue' (I.1.80).

Hotspur's sense of his own honour means he is sensitive to what he sees as others' disrespect. When he first meets the king he addresses him humbly as 'my liege' and 'your high majesty', but once Henry has criticised Mortimer, whom Hotspur regards as an honourable warrior, he swiftly loses his temper so much that his father calls him 'Drunk with choler' (anger) (I.3.127). He later risks the alliance with Glendower to ensure an equal share of the spoils. This prickliness is identified by his uncle Worcester as his main fault, and furthermore one which threatens his honourable reputation:

> Though sometimes it show greatness, courage, blood –
> And that's the dearest grace it renders you –
> Yet oftentimes it doth present harsh rage,
> Defect of manners, want of government,
> Pride, haughtiness, opinion, and disdain,
> The least of which haunting a nobleman
> Loseth men's hearts and leaves behind a stain
> Upon the beauty of all parts besides,
> Beguiling them of commendation. (III.1.175–83)

Hotspur's character is built up through his behaviour in a variety of contexts – at court and at home, with his wife or family or his enemies, but his character, unlike Hal's, remains reasonably stable throughout the play. Hotspur functions as a foil to, and exemplar for, the chameleonic (not to say calculating) Hal, and his many good qualities – including his going to battle in full knowledge that the odds are against him, but that his cause is just – help to challenge the king's simple characterisation of the Percys' actions as 'disobedience'.

HENRY IV

As the play opens, Henry appears, like the country, exhausted and drained by the civil strife preceding the play's opening. He proposes a new start, symbolised by a crusade to the Holy Land. It emerges during the scene that he has other problems too. Wales remains a problem, victories in Scotland have only led to wrangles about prisoners, his nobles appear to be plotting against him, and his eldest son Hal's deficiencies are made the more hurtful because of Hotspur's universally acknowledged abilities and honour.

Tired he may be, but Henry does not make the mistake of forgetting his royal status. In the interview with the Percys in Act I Scene 3, he peremptorily dismisses Worcester for his insolence in reminding him of his indebtedness to them. Henry's usurpation of the throne, and the role of the Percys in this, is crucial to the way the Percys see him, but we do not hear his account of it until long after Worcester has put forward the idea that he is not to be trusted. When he does eventually speak of his coming to power, in private to Hal in Act III Scene 1, he says that 'opinion' helped him get the crown. The language he uses to describe this does imply duplicity. He 'stole all courtesy from heaven', and 'dressed himself' in humility. The courtesy and humility were adopted as tactics to advance himself. But this evidence of calculation – the element of his character Worcester most fears – is to some extent offset by his admitting to a 'foolish tenderness' for his 'nearest and dearest enemy'. It is the only time the king's private emotions come through in the play, and it is placed at the point he comes closest to admitting his faults, which prevents an easy condemnation of them. But it should also not be forgotten that most of his long speech to Hal is a lesson in politics rather than an emotional appeal. Henry is at least as worried that Hal is doing himself political damage as he is concerned about personal hurt Hal has caused him.

The reconciliation between father and son at the end of Act III Scene 1 signals a change in Henry's fortunes. In public, he is the same politician, offering to be the friend of every man if they will accept his 'grace'. This offer, however genuine it may be (and Henry has not until this point shown any inclination to be friendly toward or forgive his foes) shows the king's political acumen. If it is accepted, he gains, at best, peace, and, at worst, time to prepare himself more fully to meet his enemies on ground of his choosing. Worcester's comments when discussing what he calls the king's 'kind and liberal' offer show his conviction that such a reprieve will only be temporary. Henry will 'find a time/ To punish this offence in other faults' (V.2.6–7). If the offer is rejected, however, Worcester and the others are clearly placed in the wrong.

The final battle shows both elements of Henry's character. His calculating side comes through in the conduct of the battle, in his tactic of using decoys 'disguised as the king' to confuse the enemy (and presumably to spread the morale-boosting qualities of the king's presence as much as possible). We are shown the death of one of these decoys, Sir Walter Blunt, so see the consequences of Henry's decision. But he is also shown as a father, asking Hal to leave the battle because of his wounds, proud of Lord John's steadfastness in combat against Hotspur, and pleased that Hal definitively shows his reformation by saving his life against Douglas (who in this battle is taking no prisoners).

Henry's enemies call him illegitimate and do not trust him. But whatever the status of his claim to the throne by inheritance, Henry does show kingly qualities (and in this is the opposite of Hal at the play's opening, who will inherit the crown legitimately, but who appears to lack the requisite personal qualities). He is able to use language appropriately, and knows, and is protective of, the privileges which accompany royalty. But as well as a king, he is a politician, able to size up a political situation and speak and act decisively. When he is at his most calculating, and closest to the negative picture his enemies paint of him, his relationship to Hal provides a reminder of his private side. He is a father as well as a king, and showing this enables the play to engage a sympathy for his cause which would not be so easily given had we, like the Percys, only seen his public persona.

WORCESTER

Thomas Percy, Earl of Worcester, is Northumberland's brother and Hotspur's uncle. In the first scene of the play, Westmorland tells the king that Worcester is 'Malevolent to you in all aspects' (I.1.96), and that he is behind Hotspur's keeping back of prisoners. It becomes obvious on Worcester's first appearance, in Act I Scene 3, that he is indeed plotting against the king, but he presents this to his brother and nephew as self-defence. They helped Henry to the throne, which means he fears their next move, and resents his debt to them. Worcester's first words in the play are to remind Henry of that debt, however, when he refers to Henry's greatness 'which our own hands/ Have helped to make so portly' (I.3.12–13). Worcester then does not appear again until Act III Scene 1, the scene in which the kingdom is divided up. In Act I Scene 3 he lost his patience with Hotspur, after trying to tell him, on four occassions, of his plans to oppose the king. In this scene, after Hotspur has lost his temper again, he attempts to calm him down and points out that Hotspur is 'too wilful-blame'. He agrees that this wilfulness is sometimes an asset, but insists that it 'oftentimes' leads to behaviour which could alienate 'men's hearts', and so obliterate all his virtues in the eyes of the world. As Falstaff is later to point out, honour is nothing once 'detraction' gets to work.

Before Shrewsbury, Worcester quickly sees that Northumberland's absence will damage the morale of their followers. He attempts to stop Hotspur from fighting at a disadvantage, 'The number of the King exceedeth ours./ For God's sake, cousin, stay till all come in,' III. 3. 28–9. He finally confronts the king again in Act V Scene 1, where he narrates at length how the two sides were initially allies when Richard was king, on the understanding, backed by an oath, that Henry was not seeking the crown. Henry 'forgot' his oath, and became so powerful as to threaten his former friends by 'unkind usage, dangerous countenance,/ And violation of all faith and troth/ Sworn to us in your younger enterprise' (V.1.69–71). Henry offers a general pardon, which Worcester insists is kept from Hotspur. No matter how well they behave, 'Interpretation will misquote our looks' (V.2.13). Besides, they do not have Hotspur's excuse of spontaneity, and 'we as the spring of all shall pay for all'. When Hotspur enters, Worcester tells him that the king refused to negotiate, though he does pass on Hal's offer of single combat. In his final appearance, once the battle is lost, Worcester reiterates to the king that he has been forced into action by fears for his safety.

Worcester is no Hotspur. We do not see him in battle, and he has no idealistic speeches. He is primarily a politician, insisting that he has been driven into pre-emptive action against the king by Henry's own track record of treachery, and his behaviour since becoming king. As this has already happened by the start of the play, the question of whether this is true or not remains open. His prudence is shown in his reluctance to fight at unfavourable odds and his quickness in sizing up the situation before Shrewsbury.

His decision not to tell Hotspur of Henry's offer before the battle, however, contradicts his earlier statements that Henry is equally dangerous to all the Percys, as he states without qualification that Hotspur is likely to be forgiven. His repeatedly articulated conviction that Henry is treacherous is not confirmed by any of the king's public or private speeches or actions during the play. Worcester tells the audience, and other characters in the play, that Henry is not to be trusted, but we are not shown this aspect of Henry's character. However, there is nothing explicit to support Henry's judgement that Worcester's fears are simply excuses to cover his own ambition. It is undoubtedly true, however, that Worcester denies Hotspur the chance to make peace because by the time the forces are gathered at Shrewsbury there is no turning back for him personally. This willingness to sacrifice others – particularly someone as attractive to an audience as Hotspur – to secure his own safety finally shows the Percys' rising in a negative light. This is especially so because, up until this point, Worcester's cautiousness serves to highlight Hotspur's energy and spontaneity. Worcester's clear direction of the Percy cause (though Hotspur is its figurehead) protects Hotspur from those, within the play and without, who consider rebellion one of the principal crimes.

LADY PERCY

Even more than Worcester, she throws light upon Hotspur's character. As his wife she makes claims on loyalties that he faces nowhere else and places him in private and domestic situations. She is clearly not satisfied with her role in the Percy enterprise, and her description of his sleepless nights shows that in private Hotspur has more worries and doubts about it than he admits to in public. Her question, 'Do you not love me? Do you not indeed?' (II.3.99), whether it be seen as answering Hotspur's playfulness with playfulness, or confronting his evasiveness with a blunt appeal, reminds readers and audiences of the private consequences of these public actions. In her next appearance at Act III Scene 1, she confirms Worcester's assessment of Hotspur's capriciousness, saying he is 'altogether governed by humours' (III.1.228). She functions in regard to Hotspur rather as Falstaff sometimes does in regard to Hal; both young men's characters are indicated by the tolerance and affection they inspire in others.

THEMES

GOVERNMENT AND REBELLION

The play's presentation of royalty, government and rebellion begins from a different set of assumptions to the current Western European norm. These assumptions do not always cohere, and one of the features of *Henry IV Part I* is its interest in showing how political conflict results from a clash between different ideologies of rule as well as a clash between personalities.

Politics in both Shakespeare's and Henry IV's time was a family affair. The main administrative and governmental unit was the family, and many of the most politically eminent figures were related. Historically, for example, Hotspur's wife's grandfather was the uncle of Henry IV. These interconnections are often difficult to remember, and indeed in *Henry IV Part I* Shakespeare confuses the Edmund Mortimer, proclaimed heir to Richard II, with his uncle Edmund Mortimer, who married Glendower's daughter but had no claim to the throne.

With political power being concentrated in so few hands, though in theory the monarch inherited the crown from an ancestor, in practice, for affairs to run smoothly, the opinions and interests of the greater nobility had to be considered. Henry, as king, can theoretically command. But his comments to Hal about remaining distant from the people he rules apply to him also. Worcester and Hotspur both make clear that they consider Henry IV to be one of them rather than a royal being set apart. Henry is doubly dependent, not only because the greater nobles do much of his work for him (as Hotspur does militarily) but also because they helped to place him on the throne in the first place.

'Rebellion' was another area where theory and practice sometimes diverged, as the play indicates. Though, in theory, absolute obedience is owed to the monarch, simply because he is the monarch, in practice there existed a tacit recognition that disobedience, if not outright rebellion, was a way of forcing the monarch to deal with a problem. Henry IV himself adopted this route to the crown, as Hotspur notes:

> And now forsooth takes on him to reform
>
> Some certain edicts and some strait decrees
>
> That lie too heavy on the commonwealth,
>
> Cries out upon abuses, seems to weep
>
> Over his country's wrongs ... (IV.3.78–82)

Blunt, in the same scene, treats the rising as if it were a negotiating strategy, saying that the king 'bids you name your griefs, and with all speed/ You shall have your desires with interest' (IV.3.48–9). The problem is that Henry himself has set the precedent of using this tacitly accepted manoeuvre to further personal ambition. Unsurprisingly, Henry himself is less generous at Act V Scene 1, presenting the Percys' 'griefs' as 'watercolours' to 'impaint' their cause. The issue of political disobedience in the play, then, is more complex than the simple obedience/disobedience terms in which it is sometimes described.

Honour

What honour means to Hotspur, and Hal, is clear enough. Bravery and success in battle, particularly in single combat with an equal, confer honour on the victor. Hotspur in particular equates the level of the challenge with the amount of honour gained: 'Send danger from the east unto the west,/ So honour cross it form the north to south,/ And let them grapple' (I.3.193–5). In certain circumstances, fighting bravely is more important than the end result, as Hotspur's account of Mortimer's combat with Glendower shows. In addition, treating your opponent courteously is a sign that you recognise him as an equal. But because honour is not simply dependent on a tally of victories but on the manner in which they have been gained, it is dependent (as Falstaff notes) on opinion. Honour is what the honourable think is honourable. Hotspur asks his father and uncle

> Shall it for shame be spoken in these days,
>
> Or fill up chronicles in time to come,
>
> That men of your nobility and power
>
> Did gage them both in an unjust behalf ...? (I.3.168–71)

The honour code is maintained by a self-contained 'honour community' to which its members owe their highest loyalty. Like the family, then, honour potentially cuts across loyalty to the monarch, and indeed excuses active resistance, as Hotspur shows when before Shrewsbury he says that 'the arms are fair/ When the intent of bearing them is just' (V.2.87–8). Honour makes demands on its community; as Falstaff says, it 'pricks them on'. The need to maintain reputation as a vital part of one's identity helps to explain why Henry's alleged insults are so galling, as the monarch (as at least nominal national military leader) is especially eminent in the honour community. More generally, the Percys' prior involvement in Henry's dishonourable dealings has affected their standing. Worcester notes that, suspected of involvement in Richard II's death, 'we in the world's wide mouth/ Live scandalized and foully spoken of' (I.3.151–2).

LANGUAGE

The play adheres to the Elizabethan dramatic convention that the appropriate language for commoners is prose, and the appropriate language for nobles is **blank verse** in **iambic pentameter** (lines of ten syllables, with a stress falling on every second syllable). But this is not a hard and fast distinction. Hal switches between prose and verse, depending on the situation. In Act I Scene 2 he speaks in prose until he is left alone on stage and speaks his first soliloquy – in verse. Before he and Poins rob Falstaff in Act II Scene 2 he speaks prose, but ends the scene in irregular verse. In Act II Scene 4, though he has primarily spoken in prose, he adopts blank verse to respond to the sheriff who is chasing Falstaff, switching back into prose once he has gone and he is alone with Poins. Earlier in the same scene, when he and Falstaff imitate the king, who always speaks in verse, they both use prose. Hotspur too moves between prose and verse, opening Act II Scene 3 reading aloud and commenting (in prose) on a prose letter, before switching to verse on the entry of Lady Percy, and later dropping briefly into prose at III.1.240–4. Clearly, one of the uses of the verse/prose distinction is to indicate social status. Most of the scenes in the play are wholly in one or the other, and most of the characters speak entirely in one or the other. But it is also used to indicate the relative formality or informality of a scene or part of a scene. Hotspur's prose at the end of the scene in which the 'lady sings in Welsh' clearly conveys a spontaneous and emotional reaction to his wife's refusal to sing:

> Not yours, in good sooth! Heart, you swear like a
> comfit-maker's wife – 'Not you, in good sooth!', and 'As
> true as I live', and 'As God shall mend me!', and 'As sure
> as day!'–
> And givest such sarcenet surety for thy oaths
> As if thou never walkest further than Finsbury. (III.1.241–6)

The dividing line between prose and verse is not always easy to discern. 'As if thou never walkest further than Finsbury', however you pronounce it, is an extremely irregular line. In fact, the first printing of the speech (the quarto of 1598) casts lines 241–4 as prose, while the 1623 First Folio of Shakespeare's collected works prints it as verse. At least one modern editor, David Bevington, has chosen to follow the Folio rather than quarto arrangement, and print the speech as verse, beginning lines at 'Not', 'Heart', 'Not' and 'And'.

The shift from prose to verse can indicate an increase in formality or restraint on the part of the speaker. The best example of this comes at Act I Scene 2, where Hal drops the prose he has been using with the commoners, revealing his plans, in a blank verse soliloquy, to abandon his companions, when it suits him. The use of verse and prose is, however, just one example of the way Shakespeare provides his characters with different kinds of language to suit their personality, role and situation.

Prose is particularly suited to producing the illusion of realism, as it is closer to the rhythms of speech than a regular metre is. A good example is the hostess's emotional protest to Falstaff, which in its use of repetition and its simple grammar gives the impression of breathless indignation, nicely rendered by the Penguin editor's decision to punctuate it all as one sentence: 'No, Sir John, you do not know me, Sir John, I know you, Sir John, you owe me money, Sir John, and now you pick a quarrel to beguile me of it' (III.3.64–6). But this relative closeness to speech is not to say that prose is simpler or less subtle than verse. At the other end of the spectrum from the hostess, Hal and Falstaff use prose in highly controlled and inventive ways, showing how repetition, variation and figurative language are not confined to verse. An example is Falstaff's indignant response in Act II Scene 4 to Hal's request that he explain how he could see knaves dressed in Kendal green if it was too dark to see his hand:

> What, upon compulsion? Zounds, an I were at the
> strappado, or all the racks in the world, I would not tell
> you on compulsion. Give you a reason on compulsion? If
> reasons were as plentiful as blackberries, I would give no
> man a reason upon compulsion, I. (II.4.232–6)

The repetitions of 'upon/on compulsion' in various contexts in this short speech shows how Falstaff structures his response for effect, able to communicate his point effectively whilst avoiding simple repetition. In fact, variation on a theme is one of Falstaff's characteristic linguistic strategies, one also adopted by Hal. As many critics have noted, both Hal and Falstaff are improvisers, working quickly and intuitively to respond to whatever cues the situation, or the last person to speak to them, might throw up. Their language, particularly when they are together, has a playful and improvisatory quality. They feed each other's ingenuity. As with any pattern, deviation from this usual way of interacting can be used for effect. When Falstaff drops his usual habit of banter to say to Hal 'I would 'twere bed-time, Hal, and all well' before the battle (V.1.125), the change in his language highlights the presence of a different Falstaff.

The play's use of verse is also context-specific. King Henry's first speech in the play is a piece of formal rhetoric, grammatically complex and dense with images, giving the impression of a disciplined imagination revealing itself not just through what is said, but through the way that it is said:

> So shaken as we are, so wan with care,
> Find we a time for frighted peace to pant,
> And breathe short-winded accents of new broils
> To be commenced in strands afar remote.
> No more the thirsty entrance of this soil
> Shall daub her lips with her own children's blood,
> No more shall trenching war channel her fields,
> Nor bruise her flowerets with the armèd hoofs
> Of hostile paces. (I.1.1–9)

These lines show how metre, the defining feature of verse, can help to emphasise certain words. By diverging from the usual order of words, the first two lines ensure that certain key words are emphasised – shaken, wan, care, frighted, peace, pant. The predominance of monosyllables in these two lines also enables a regular metrical pattern to be set up. Though there are places in the speech where an actor might break up the regularity of the metre for effect – for example, 'Find we' (line 2) could easily stress the first rather than the second syllable, which would break the flow – there is only one place in these lines where the metre is disrupted. This regularity helps to give the impression of a controlled utterance. But precisely because the speech is so regular metrically, the word 'channel' stands out, drawing attention to the way in which 'trenching war' cuts through the land. Similarly, the way the speech uses words out of the usual order gives the impression of a self-conscious piece of rhetoric. The usual word ordering in line 7 would give us 'trenching war shall channel her fields no more'. Without metre, the word 'channel' has no particular emphasis. The line no longer starts with a negative, which has much more emphasis in Shakespeare's ordering (thus indicating that the important thing about the war is that it has stopped, not that it is 'trenching').

PART FOUR

TEXTUAL ANALYSIS

TEXT 1   Hotspur and Lady Percy (II.3.1–67)

HOTSPUR: *But for mine own part, my lord, I could be well*
contented to be there, in respect of the love I bear your
house.
He could be contented! Why is he not then? In respect
of the love he bears our house? He shows in this he
loves his own barn better than he loves our house. Let
me see some more.
The purpose you undertake is dangerous,
Why, that's certain. 'Tis dangerous to take a cold, to
sleep, to drink. But I tell you, my lord fool, out of this   10
nettle, danger, we pluck this flower, safety.
The purpose you undertake is dangerous, the friends you
have named uncertain, the time itself unsorted, and your
whole plot too light, for the counterpoise of so great an
opposition.
Say you so, say you so? I say unto you again, you are a
shallow cowardly hind, and you lie. What a lack-brain is
this! By the Lord, our plot is a good plot, as ever was
laid, our friends true and constant. A good plot, good
friends, and full of expectation. An excellent plot, very   20
good friends. What a frosty-spirited rogue is this! Why,
my Lord of York commends the plot, and the general
course of the action. Zounds, an I were now by this
rascal I could brain him with his lady's fan. Is there not
my father, my uncle, and myself? Lord Edmund
Mortimer, my Lord of York, and Owen Glendower? Is
there not besides the Douglas? Have I not all their
letters to meet me in arms by the ninth of the next
month, and are they not some of them set forward

already? What a pagan rascal is this, an infidel! Ha!   30
You shall see now in very sincerity of fear and cold heart
will he to the King, and lay open all our proceedings!
O, I could divide myself, and go to buffets, for moving
such a dish of skim milk with so honourable an action!
Hang him, let him tell the King, we are prepared. I will
set forward tonight.

        Enter his lady

How now, Kate? I must leave you within these two
hours.

LADY PERCY: O my good lord, why are you thus alone?
For what offence have I this fortnight been   40
A banished woman from my Harry's bed?
Tell me, sweet lord, what is it that takes from thee
Thy stomach, pleasure, and they golden sleep?
Why dost thou bend thine eyes upon the earth,
And start so often when thou sittest alone?
Why hast thou lost the fresh blood in thy cheeks,
And given my treasures and my rights of thee
To thick-eyed musing, and curst melancholy?
In thy faint slumbers I by thee have watched
And heard thee murmur tales of iron wars,   50
Speak terms of manage to thy bounding steed,
Cry 'Courage! To the field!' And thou hast talked
Of sallies, and retires, of trenches, tents,
Of palisadoes, frontiers, parapets,
Of basilisks, of cannon, culverin,
Of prisoners' ransom, and of soldiers slain,
And all the currents of a heady fight.
Thy spirit within thee hath been so at war,
And thus hath so bestirred thee in thy sleep,
That beads of sweat have stood upon thy brow   60
Like bubbles in a late-disturbèd stream,
And in thy face strange motions have appeared,
Such as we see when men restrain their breath
On some great sudden hest. O, what portents are these?

> Some heavy business hath my lord in hand,
> And I must know it, else he loves me not.

HOTSPUR: What ho!

At the end of Act I Scene 3 it appears that Worcester has already carefully prepared the ground for the Percy plot against the king, and that Henry IV's throne is in immediate danger. Here, it becomes apparent that this is not so, as Hotspur reads out a letter from an unnamed ally, commenting upon it as he does so. One of the technical challenges facing Shakespeare in this play is to suggest a private side to his characters when the action is primarily public. One of the most common and effective ways of doing this is via **soliloquy**, but this suits some character types more than others. Harry Hotspur is not, as Falstaff and Prince Hal both are, a natural commentator on events. Nor is he, as both the prince and Falstaff are, self-conscious about the roles he adopts. By this point, the comparison between Hotspur and Prince Hal has been well established, and Hal has been shown to be a consummate role-player, ending Act I Scene 2 stepping from one persona into its opposite. The challenge facing Shakespeare was to suggest how Hotspur's private and public selves are the same, and to clearly show that Hotspur does not adopt roles as Hal does. Hotspur's primary characteristic for much of the play is his hot-temperedness. In a political world where the main actors – Henry IV and Worcester – are calculating politicians, this spontaneity is an attractive trait. The device of Hotspur reading aloud and commenting on a letter establishes Hotspur's volatility, in his second appearance on stage, as an essential part of his personality rather than simply being a role he plays. It clearly delineates the difference between himself and Hal.

Hotspur conducts a kind of dialogue with the words he reads out, repeating and commenting upon them, combatively picking up phrases for special attention as he does in conversation with others: 'He could be contented! Why is he not then?' (II.3.4). His spontaneity shows itself in the repetitions and circularities of his responses, which clearly indicate an informal and unstructured mind at work: 'By the Lord, our plot is a good plot, as ever was laid, our friends true and constant. A good plot, good friends, and full of expectation. An excellent plot, very good friends' (II.3.18–21). He speaks in a prose reflecting the rhythms of speech. His characterisation of the letter-writer ('a frosty-spirited rogue', 'this rascal', 'a pagan rascal ... an infidel', 'such a dish of skim milk') confirms the pugnacious side to his character already displayed in his response to the king's characterisation of Mortimer in Act I Scene 3.

That these qualities add up to a lack of self-knowledge in Hotspur has already been suggested by his uncle's and father's irritation with him. Lady Percy's long speech to him confirms that Hotspur's subconscious response to the situation is very different to the one he has just presented. Through this description of Hotspur's involuntary movements, general moods and behaviour whilst dreaming Shakespeare manages to suggest another side to Hotspur than the one he is himself aware of. He is alternately jumpy and pensive when alone. At night, he has 'faint slumbers' rather than 'golden sleep'. Though he is recognised as pre-eminent in battle throughout the play, in his dreams of fighting he shows no enjoyment. Dreams of war mean that 'Thy spirit within thee hath been ... at war' (II.3.58). In an image vividly summing up this inner turbulence, Lady Percy compares his sweat to the bubbles produced by a disturbed stream.

Lady Percy's speech clearly indicates her husband's state of mind and, almost in passing, her own pain ('For what offence have I this fortnight been/ A banished woman?', II.3.40–1). His response to it shows he does recognise, or want to recognise, this state of affairs. Instead of responding to her directly, a mode already established as his habitual way of speaking, he changes the subject and asks a servant about letters and horses. Suddenly the character seemingly incapable of calculation becomes transparently insincere and evasive. Lady Percy's evidence that he is taking the rising much more seriously than his commentary on the letter might indicate also serves to show his impetuousness as having complex roots, and so adds to the character's psychological depth.

TEXT 2   Henry IV on his coming to power (III.2.29–91)

KING HENRY:

God pardon thee! Yet let me wonder, Harry,
At thy affections, which do hold a wing   30
Quite from the flight of all thy ancestors.
Thy place in Council thou hast rudely lost,
Which by thy younger brother is supplied,
And art almost an alien to the hearts
Of all the court and princes of my blood.

The hope and expectation of thy time
Is ruined, and the soul of every man
Prophetically do forethink thy fall.
Had I so lavish of my presence been,
So common-hackneyed in the eyes of men,   40
So stale and cheap to vulgar company,
Opinion, that did help me to the crown,
Had still kept loyal to possession,
And left me in reputeless banishment,
A fellow of no mark nor likelihood.
By being seldom seen, I could not stir
But like a comet I was wondered at,
That men would tell their children, 'This is he!'
Others would say, 'Where, which is Bolingbroke?'
And then I stole all courtesy from heaven,   50
And dressed myself in such humility
That I did pluck allegiance from men's hearts,
Loud shouts and salutations from their mouths,
Even in the presence of the crownèd King.
Thus did I keep my person fresh and new,
My presence, like a robe pontifical,
Ne'er seen but wondered at, and so my state,
Seldom, but sumptuous, showed like a feast,
And won by rareness such solemnity.
The skipping King, he ambled up and down,   60
With shallow jesters, and rash bavin wits,
Soon kindled and soon burnt, carded his state,
Mingled his royalty with capering fools,
Had his great name profanèd with their scorns,
And gave his countenance against his name
To laugh at gibing boys, and stand the push
Of every beardless vain comparative,
Grew a companion to the common streets,
Enfeoffed himself to popularity,
That, being daily swallowed by men's eyes,   70
They surfeited with honey, and began
To loathe the taste of sweetness, whereof a little

More than a little is by much too much.
So, when he had occasion to be seen,
He was but as the cuckoo is in June,
Heard, not regarded; seen, but with such eyes
As, sick and blunted with community,
Afford no extraordinary gaze,
Such as is bent on sun-like majesty
When it shines seldom in admiring eyes,   80
But rather drowsed and hung their eyelids down,
Slept in his face, and rendered such aspect
As cloudy men use to their adversaries,
Being with his presence glutted, gorged, and full.
And in that very line, Harry, standest thou,
For thou hast lost thy princely privilege
With vile participation. Not an eye
But is a-weary of thy common sight,
Save mine, which hath desired to see thee more,
Which now doth that I would not have it do,   90
Make blind itself with foolish tenderness.

This long speech by King Henry has a number of functions. It shows the king's private feelings for his son, which gives some sense of a character behind the kingly role. It is also an extended explanation of just what the kingly role is, largely through a description of what it is not. Though the scene shows the king in private, his criticism of Hal's wildness does not need closed doors. He has already made public his feelings on his son's irresponsibility. What has not – and will not – surface outside this private interview is Henry's extended musings upon the arts needed to gain and maintain a crown. Appropriately, this 'private' topic is the public presentation of royalty. 'Opinion', Henry bluntly states, 'did help me to the crown'. Royalty should be rarely seen, and, when seen, solemn. The mistake of Richard II, which Hal is repeating, was to tarnish his state by associating with 'capering fools', 'shallow jesters' and 'rash bavin wits', and to appear in public too often. Henry here is, in effect, defining what legitimates a monarch. Obedience is produced rather than innate, from the highest to the lowest, and order must continually be remade. Decorum is an essential component of legitimate power. Hal must keep apart from the people for decorum's sake rather than indulge in 'vile participation' (vile here primarily referring to the social distinctions between nobles and 'villeins'). Monarchy is weakened by association with the people. It is also weakened, theatrically speaking, by contact with **comedy**. It is no coincidence that Hal's last scene was spent in the company of a superb jester, fool, and wit. If Hal really is, as he claims, learning the language of the commons during his time in the tavern, then the actual evidence of this in performance is in his exercise of verbal wit. Hal can be comic: but twice already in the play he has consciously switched a scene away from the comic, in his **soliloquy** at the end of Act 1 Scene 2, and his impersonation of his father in Act 2 Scene 4. As the play progresses his sense of humour diverges from Falstaff's, something which Falstaff's presence on the battlefield – where Hal is in deadly earnest – helps to highlight.

TEXT 3   The death of Hotspur and the resurrection of Falstaff (V.4.76–127)

HOTSPUR:

O Harry, thou hast robbed me of my youth!
I better brook the loss of brittle life
Than those proud titles thou hast won of me.
They wound my thoughts worse than thy sword my
    flesh.
But thoughts, the slaves of life, and life, time's fool,   80
And time, that takes survey of all the world,
Must have a stop. O, I could prophesy,
But that the earthy and cold hand of death
Lies on my tongue. No, Percy, thou art dust,
And food for –

                         He dies

PRINCE HAL:

For worms, brave Percy. Fare thee well, great heart!
Ill-weaved ambition, how much art thou shrunk.
When that this body did contain a spirit,
A kingdom for it was too small a bound.
But now two paces of the vilest earth   90
Is room enough. This earth that bears thee dead
Bears not alive so stout a gentleman.

If thou wert sensible of courtesy
I should not make so dear a show of zeal,
But let my favours hide thy mangled face,
And even in thy behalf I'll thank myself
For doing these fair rites of tenderness.
Adieu, and take thy praise with thee to heaven!
Thy ignominy sleep with thee in the grave,
But not remembered in thy epitaph.   100
    He spieth Falstaff on the ground
What, old acquaintance, could not all this flesh
Keep in a little life? Poor Jack, farewell!
I could have better spared a better man.
O, I should have a heavy miss of thee
If I were much in love with vanity.
Death hath not struck so fat a deer today,
Though many dearer, in this bloody fray.
Embowelled will I see thee by and by,
Till then in blood by noble Percy lie.   *Exit*
    Falstaff riseth up

FALSTAFF: Embowelled? If thou embowel me today, I'll   110
give you leave to powder me and eat me too tomorrow.
'Sblood, 'twas time to counterfeit, or that hot termagant
Scot had paid me, scot and lot too. Counterfeit? I lie,
I am no counterfeit. To die is to be counterfeit, for he
is but the counterfeit of a man who hath not the life of
a man. But to counterfeit dying, when a man thereby
liveth, is to be no counterfeit, but the true and perfect
image of life indeed. The better part of valour is dis-
cretion, in the which better part I have saved my life.
Zounds, I am afraid of this gunpowder Percy, though he   120
be dead. How if he should counterfeit too and rise? By
my faith, I am afraid he would prove the better counterfeit. Therefore, I'll make him sure, yea, and I'll swear I
killed him. Why may not he rise as well as I? Nothing
confutes me but eyes, and nobody sees me. Therefore,
sirrah (*stabbing him*), with a new wound in your thigh,
come you along with me.

In these few lines the play reaches its climax as Hotspur dies and Falstaff rises again. These three tremendously varied set speeches engage a wide range of responses, from the serious to the comic. It was a convention in the Elizabethan theatre that dying speeches, as farewells to the world, in some sense sum up the dying person. In addition, dying speeches were often associated with prophecy, as if insight to the future came with closeness to an afterlife. Hotspur's dying speech is particularly effective because it is so different to the way he habitually speaks. Throughout the play Hotspur has characteristically been upbeat, combative, spontaneous and informal; here he is measured, grave, philosophical and hopeless. He has lost both life and that which is dearer to him than life, his 'proud titles'.

The section begins with a characteristic informality ('O Harry'), and continues into Hotspur's shocked accusation that he has been robbed not of his life, but of his youth. This reminds audience and reader of his age, and heightens the sense of waste produced by his death. Hotspur then reiterates one of the play's typical oppositions, between physical and mental damage: defeat in battle means that his martial honour is lost to Hal, which is the deepest loss he can feel. As he approaches death, he recognises that thoughts are subject to life, and must stop; that life itself is subject to time, and must also end; and finally, that even time will come to an end. This uncharacteristically philosophical note is followed by an equally out of character recognition that he would speak as a prophet had his time not run out. His final, incomplete, sentence, again uncharacteristically, addresses himself, as reduced from the height of chivalry to dust.

Hal's speech, which follows directly on, divides into two, focused on Hotspur and Falstaff respectively. Unlike Hotspur, Hal does not behave out of character here, but the speech is important in confirming just what his character now is. At the play's opening Hal seemed divided between an Eastcheap inhabitant and a prince-to-be, with no clear way of bridging the gap between the two. Here he speaks clearly as someone who has thrown off the 'loose behaviour' which caused Hotspur to scoff at him.

Hal's **eulogy** for Hotspur is somewhat qualified. On the one hand, he calls him 'great heart' and refers to his performance of 'these fair rites of tenderness'. On the other hand, for each positive mention of Hotspur there is a negative: 'ill-weaved ambition', or 'thy ignominy'. Hal, the inheritor of Hotspur's honour, is also the inheritor of Henry IV's throne, and takes Henry's unforgiving perspective on 'rebellion'. The vacillation of this

PART FIVE

BACKGROUND

WILLIAM SHAKESPEARE'S LIFE

There are no personal records of Shakespeare's life. Official documents and occasional references to him by contemporary dramatists enable us to draw the main outline of his public life, but his private life remains hidden. Although not at all unusual for a writer of his time, this lack of first-hand evidence has tempted many to read his plays as personal records and to look in them for clues to Shakespeare's character and convictions. The results are unconvincing, partly because Renaissance art was not subjective or designed primarily to express its creator's personality, and partly because the drama of any period is very difficult to read biographically. Except when plays are written by committed dramatists to promote social or political causes (as by Shaw or Brecht), it is all but impossible to decide who amongst the variety of fictional characters in a drama represents the dramatist, or which of the various and often conflicting points of view expressed is authorial.

What we do know can be quickly summarised. Shakespeare was born into a well-to-do family in the market town of Stratford-upon-Avon in Warwickshire, where he was baptised, in Holy Trinity Church, on 26 April 1564. His father, John Shakespeare, was a prosperous glover and leather merchant who became a person of some importance in the town: in 1565 he was elected an alderman of the town, and in 1568 he became high bailiff (or mayor) of Stratford. In 1557 he had married Mary Arden. Their third child (of eight) and eldest son, William, learned to read and write at the primary (or 'petty') school in Stratford and then, it seems probable, attended the local grammar school, where he would have studied Latin, history, logic and rhetoric. In November 1582 William, then aged eighteen, married Anne Hathaway, who was twenty-six years old. They had a daughter, Susanna, in May 1583, and twins, Hamnet and Judith, in 1585.

Shakespeare next appears in the historical record in 1592 when he was mentioned as a London actor and playwright in a pamphlet by the dramatist Robert Greene. These 'lost years' 1585–92 have been the subject of much speculation, but how they were occupied remains as much a mystery as when Shakespeare left Stratford, and why. In his pamphlet, *Greene's Groatsworth of Wit*, Greene expresses to his fellow dramatists his outrage that the 'upstart crow' Shakespeare has the impudence to believe he 'is as well able to bombast out a **blank verse** as the best of you'. To have aroused this hostility from a rival, Shakespeare must, by 1592, have been long enough in London to have made a name for himself as a playwright. We may conjecture that he had left Stratford in 1586 or 1587.

During the next twenty years, Shakespeare continued to live in London, regularly visiting his wife and family in Stratford. He continued to act, but his chief fame was as a dramatist. From 1594 he wrote exclusively for the Lord Chamberlain's Men, which rapidly became the leading dramatic company and from 1603 enjoyed the patronage of James I as the King's Men. His plays were extremely popular and he became a shareholder in his theatre company. He was able to buy lands around Stratford and a large house in the town, to which he retired about 1611. He died there on 23 April 1616 and was buried in Holy Trinity Church on 25 April.

SHAKESPEARE'S DRAMATIC CAREER

Between the late 1580s and 1613 Shakespeare wrote thirty-seven plays, and contributed to some by other dramatists. This was by no means an exceptional number for a professional playwright of the times. The exact date of the composition of individual plays is a matter of debate – for only a few plays is the date of their first performance known – but the broad outlines of Shakespeare's dramatic career have been established. He began in the late 1580s and early 1590s by rewriting earlier plays and working with plotlines inspired by the Classics. He concentrated on comedies (such as *The Comedy of Errors*, 1590–4, which derived from the Latin playwright Plautus) and plays dealing with English history (such as the three parts of *Henry VI*, 1589–92), though he also tried his hand at bloodthirsty revenge tragedy (*Titus Andronicus*, 1592–3, indebted to both Ovid and Seneca). During the 1590s Shakespeare developed his expertise in these kinds of play to write such comic masterpieces such as *A Midsummer Night's Dream* (1594–5) and *As You Like It* (1599–1600) and history plays such as *Henry IV* (1596–8) and *Henry V* (1598–9).

As the new century begins a new note is detectable. Plays such as *Troilus and Cressida* (1601–2) and *Measure for Measure* (1603–4), poised between **comedy** and **tragedy**, evoke complex responses. Because of their generic uncertainty and ambivalent tone such works are sometimes referred to as 'problem plays', but it is tragedy which comes to dominate the extraordinary sequence of masterpieces: *Hamlet* (1600–1), *Othello* (1602–4), *King Lear* (1605–6), *Macbeth* (1605–6) and *Antony and Cleopatra* (1606).

In the last years of his dramatic career, Shakespeare wrote a group of plays of a quite different kind. These 'romances', as they are often called, are in many ways the most remarkable of all his plays. The group comprises *Pericles* (1608), *Cymbeline* (1609–11), *The Winter's Tale* (1610–11) and *The Tempest* (1610–11). These plays (particularly *Cymbeline*) reprise many of the situations and themes of the earlier dramas but in fantastical and exotic dramatic designs which, set in distant lands, covering large tracts of time and involving music, mime, dance and tableaux, have something of the qualities of masques and pageants. The situations which in the tragedies had led to disaster are here resolved: the great theme is restoration and reconciliation. Where in the tragedies Ophelia, Desdemona and Cordelia died, the daughters of these plays – Marina, Imogen, Perdita, Miranda – survive and are reunited with their parents and lovers.

THE TEXTS OF SHAKESPEARE'S PLAYS

Nineteen of Shakespeare's plays were printed during his lifetime in what are called 'quartos' from the fact that these books, which each contained one play, were made up of sheets of paper each folded twice to make four leaves. Shakespeare, however, did not supervise the publication of these plays. This was not unusual. When a playwright had sold a play to a dramatic company he sold his rights in it: copyright belonged to whoever had possession of an actual copy of the text, and so consequently authors had no control over what happened their work. Anyone who could get hold of the text of a play might publish it if they wished. Hence, what found its way into print might be the author's copy, but it might be an actor's copy or prompt copy, perhaps cut or altered for performance; sometimes, actors (or even members of the audience) might publish what they could remember of the text. Printers, working without the benefit of the author's oversight, introduced their own errors, through misreading the manuscript for example, and by 'correcting' what seemed to them not to make sense.

In 1623 John Heminges and Henry Condell, two actors in Shakespeare's company, collected together texts of thirty-six of Shakespeare's plays (*Pericles* was omitted) and published them in a large folio (a book in which each sheet of paper is folded once in half, to give two leaves). This, the First Folio, was followed by later editions in 1632, 1663 and 1685. Despite its appearance of authority, however, the texts in the First Folio still present many difficulties, for there are printing errors and confused passages in the plays, and its texts often differ significantly from those of the earlier quartos, when these exist.

Shakespeare's texts have, then, been through a number of intermediaries. We do not have his authority for any one of his plays, and hence we cannot know exactly what it was that he wrote. Bibliographers, textual critics and editors have spent a great deal of effort on endeavouring to get behind the errors, uncertainties and contradictions in the available texts to recover the plays as Shakespeare originally wrote them. What we read is the result of these efforts. Modern texts are what editors have constructed from the available evidence: they correspond to no sixteenth or seventeenth-century editions, and to no early performance of a Shakespeare play. Furthermore, these composite texts differ from each other, for different editors read the early texts differently and come to different conclusions. A Shakespeare text is an unstable and a contrived thing.

Often, of course, its judgements embody, if not the personal prejudices of the editor, then the cultural preferences of the time in which he or she was working. Growing awareness of this has led recent scholars to distrust the whole editorial enterprise and to repudiate the attempt to construct a 'perfect' text. Stanley Wells and Gary Taylor, the editors of the Oxford edition of *The Complete Works* (1988), point out that almost certainly the texts of Shakespeare's plays were altered in performance, and from one performance to another, so that there may never have been a single version. They note, too, that Shakespeare probably revised and rewrote some plays. They do not claim to print a definitive text of any play, but prefer what seems to them the 'more theatrical' version, and when there is a great difference between available versions, as with *King Lear*, they print two texts.

Shakespeare arrived in London at the very time that the Elizabethan period was poised to become the 'golden age' of English literature. Although Elizabeth reigned as queen from 1558 to 1603, the term 'Elizabethan' is used very loosely in a literary sense to refer to the period 1580 to 1625, when the great works of the age were produced. (Sometimes the later part of this period is distinguished as 'Jacobean', from the Latin form of the name of the king who succeeded Elizabeth, James I of England and VI of Scotland, who reigned from 1603 to 1625.) The poet Edmund Spenser heralded this new age with his pastoral poem *The Shepheardes Calender* (1579) and in his essay *An Apologie for Poetrie* (written about 1580, although not published until 1595) his friend Sir Philip Sidney championed the imaginative power of the 'speaking picture of poesy', famously declaring that 'Nature never set forth the earth in so rich a tapestry as divers poets have done ... Her world is brazen, the poet's only deliver a golden'.

Spenser and Sidney were part of that rejuvenating movement in European culture which since the nineteenth century has been known by the term *Renaissance*. Meaning literally *rebirth* it denotes a revival and redirection of artistic and intellectual endeavour which began in Italy in the fourteenth century in the poetry of Petrarch. It spread gradually northwards across Europe, and is first detectable in England in the early sixteenth century in the writings of the scholar and statesman Sir Thomas More and in the poetry of Sir Thomas Wyatt and Henry Howard, Earl of Surrey. Its keynote was a readiness to challenge old assumptions and traditions. To the innovative spirit of the Renaissance, the preceding ages appeared dully unoriginal and conformist.

That spirit was fuelled by the rediscovery of many Classical texts and the culture of Greece and Rome. This fostered a confidence in human reason and in human potential which, in every sphere, challenged old convictions. The European discovery of America and its peoples (Columbus had sailed in 1492) demonstrated that the world was a larger and stranger place than had been thought. The cosmological speculation of Copernicus (later confirmed by Galileo) that the sun, not the earth was the centre of our planetary system challenged the centuries-old belief that the earth and human beings were at the centre of the cosmos. The pragmatic political philosophy of Machiavelli seemed to cut politics free from its traditional link with morality by permitting to statesmen any means which secured the desired end. And the religious movements we know collectively as the Reformation broke with the Church of Rome and set the individual conscience, not ecclesiastical authority, at the centre of the religious life. Nothing, it seemed, was beyond questioning, nothing impossible.

Shakespeare's drama is innovative and challenging in exactly the way of the Renaissance. It interrogates (examines and asks questions of) the beliefs, assumptions and politics upon which Elizabethan society was founded. And although the plays generally conclude in a restoration of order and stability, many critics are inclined to argue that their imaginative energy goes into subverting, rather than reinforcing, traditional values. They would point out that the famous speech on hierarchical order in *Troilus and Cressida* (I.3.86–124) or Katerina's speech on wifely submission to patriarchal authority in *The Taming of the Shrew* (V.2.146–60) appear to be rendered **ironic** by the action of the plays in which they occur. Convention, audience expectation and, perhaps, the existence of theatrical censorship all required the status quo to be endorsed by the plots' conclusions, but the dramas find ways to allow alternative sentiments to be expressed. Frequently, figures of authority are undercut by some comic or parodic figure: against the Duke in *Measure for Measure* is set Lucio; against Prospero in *The Tempest*, Caliban; against Henry IV, of course, Falstaff. Despairing, critical, dissident, disillusioned, unbalanced, rebellious, mocking voices are repeatedly to be heard in the plays, rejecting, resenting, defying the established order. They belong always to figures marginalized by social class, or gender, or race, 'licensed', as it were, by their situations on the edges of power to say what would be unacceptable from socially privileged or responsible citizens. The question is: are such characters given these views to discredit them, or were they the only ones through whom a voice could be given to radical and dissident ideas? It is a question to which criticism of *Henry IV Part I* keeps returning.

Renaissance culture was intensely nationalistic. With the break-up of the internationalism of the Middle Ages the evolving nation states which still mark the map of Europe began for the first time to acquire distinctive cultural identities. There was intense rivalry among them as they sought to achieve in their own vernacular languages a culture which could equal that of Greece and Rome. Spenser's great allegorical epic poem *The Faerie Queene*, which began to appear from 1590, celebrated Elizabeth and was intended to outdo the poetic achievements of France and Italy and to stand beside Virgil and Homer. Shakespeare's history plays share this preoccupation with national identity. They show how modern England came into being, through the conflicts of the fifteenth-century Wars of the Roses which brought the Tudors to the throne. He is fascinated, too, by the related subject of politics and the exercise of power. With the collapse of medieval feudalism and the authority of local barons, the royal court in the Renaissance came to assume a new status as the centre of power and patronage. It was here that the destiny of a country was shaped. *Henry IV Part I* shows that this assumption of power, and, more importantly, legitimacy, by such a centralised authority did not go uncontested.

By Shakespeare's own time, power was much more centred on the court than in the period covered in *Henry IV Part I*. That is why we are usually at court in his plays, and in the company of courtiers. But the dramatic gaze is not merely admiring; through a variety of devices, a critical perspective is brought to bear. This is particularly true of *Henry IV Part I*, in which the court is paralleled and challenged by a very different world, rooted in a different code of values. More generally, the court's hypocrisy may be bitterly denounced (for example, in the diatribes of the mad Lear) and its self-seeking ambition represented disturbingly in the figure of a machiavellian villain (such as Edmund in *Lear*) or a malcontent (such as Iago in *Othello*). Shakespeare is fond of displacing the court to another context, the better to examine its assumptions and pretensions and to offer alternatives to the courtly life (for example, in the pastoral setting of the forest of Arden in *As You Like It* or Prospero's island in *The Tempest*). Courtiers are frequently figures of fun whose unmanly sophistication ('neat and trimly dressed/ Fresh as a bridegroom ... perfumed like a milliner' says Hotspur of such a man in *Henry IV Part I*, I.3.32–5) is contrasted with plain-speaking integrity: Oswald is set against Kent in *King Lear*. When considering the elements of critique in Shakespeare's plays, we should not forget that both print and theatres were subject to scrutiny, print by the church and the theatre by a court official known as the Master of the Revels. We have some manuscripts of plays returned to theatre companies by the Master of the Revels with instructions for amendments and cuts still visible. It was understood that certain topics were not usually safe to handle, in particular the direct representation of those in power. This has something to do with why our plays tend to be set either in the past, or abroad. It should also be remembered that theatre companies were technically servants of nobles. This status allowed them freedom of movement when touring, and gave them access to lucrative command performances at court and elsewhere. Shakespeare's company was initially known as the Lord Chamberlain's Men and after the accession to the throne of James VI of Scotland became the King's Men.

The nationalism of the English Renaissance was reinforced by Protestantism. Henry VIII had broken with Rome in the 1530s and in Shakespeare's time there was an independent Protestant state church. Because the Pope in Rome had excommunicated Queen Elizabeth as a heretic and relieved the English of their allegiance to the crown, there was deep suspicion of Roman Catholics as potential traitors. This was enforced by the attempted invasion of the Spanish Armada in 1588. This was a religiously inspired crusade to overthrow Elizabeth and restore England to Roman Catholic allegiance. Roman Catholicism was hence easily identified with hostility to England. Its association with disloyalty and treachery was enforced by the Gunpowder Plot of 1605, a Roman Catholic attempt to destroy the government of England.

Shakespeare's plays are remarkably free from direct religious sentiment, but their emphases are Protestant. Young women, for example, are destined for marriage, not for nunneries (precisely what Isabella appears to escape at the end of *Measure for Measure*); friars are dubious characters, full of schemes and deceptions, if with benign intentions, as in *Much Ado About Nothing* or *Romeo and Juliet*. (We should add, though, that Puritans, extreme Protestants, are even less kindly treated: for example, Malvolio in *Twelfth Night*). The central figures of the plays are frequently individuals beset by temptation, by the lure of evil – Angelo in *Measure for Measure*, Othello, Lear, Macbeth – and not only in tragedies: Falstaff is described as 'that old white-bearded Satan' (*Henry IV Part I* II.4.450). We follow their inner struggles. Shakespeare's heroes have the preoccupation with self and the introspective tendencies encouraged by Protestantism: his tragic heroes are haunted by their consciences, seeking their true selves, agonising over what course of action to take as they follow what can often be understood as a kind of spiritual progress towards heaven or hell.

The theatre for which the plays were written was one of the most remarkable innovations of the Renaissance. There had been no professional theatres or acting companies during the medieval period. Performed on carts and in open spaces at Christian festivals, plays had been almost exclusively religious. Such professional actors as there were wandered the country putting on a variety of entertainments in the yards of inns, on make-shift stages in market squares, or anywhere else suitable. They did not perform full-length plays, but mimes, juggling and **comedy** acts. Such actors were regarded by officialdom and polite society as little better than vagabonds and layabouts.

Just before Shakespeare went to London all this began to change. A number of young men who had been to the universities of Oxford and Cambridge came to London in the 1580s and began to write plays which made use of what they had learned about the Classical drama of ancient Greece and Rome. Plays such as John Lyly's *Alexander and Campaspe* (1584), Christopher Marlowe's *Tamburlaine the Great* (about 1587) and Thomas Kyd's *The Spanish Tragedy* (1588–9) were unlike anything that had been written in English before. They were full-length plays on secular subjects, taking their plots from history and legend, adopting many of the devices of Classical drama, and offering a range of characterisation and situation hitherto unattempted in English drama. With the exception of Lyly's prose dramas, they were composed in the unrhymed iambic pentameters (**blank verse**) which the Earl of Surrey had introduced into English earlier in the sixteenth century. This was a freer and more expressive medium than the rhymed verse of medieval drama. It was the drama of these 'university wits' which Shakespeare challenged when he came to London. Greene was one of them, and we have heard how little he liked this Shakespeare setting himself up as a dramatist.

The most significant change of all, however, was that these dramatists wrote for the professional theatre. In 1576 James Burbage built the first permanent theatre in England, in Shoreditch, just beyond London's northern boundary. It was called simply 'The Theatre'. Others soon followed. Thus, when Shakespeare came to London, there was a flourishing drama, theatres and companies of actors waiting for him, such as there had never been before in England. His company performed at James Burbage's Theatre until 1596, and used the Swan and Curtain until they moved into their own new theatre, the Globe, in 1599. It was burned

THE GLOBE THEATRE,

On the 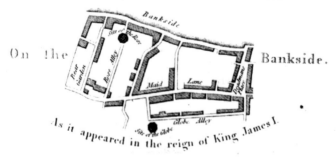 Bankside.

As it appeared in the reign of King James I.

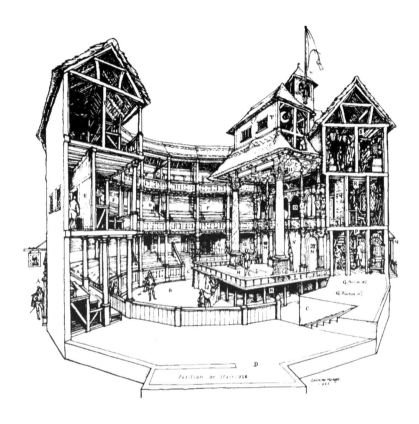

A CONJECTURAL RECONSTRUCTION OF THE INTERIOR OF THE GLOBE PLAYHOUSE

AA Main entrance
B The Yard
CC Entrances to lowest galleries
D Entrance to staircase and upper galleries
E Corridor serving the different sections of the middle gallery
F Middle gallery ('Twopenny Rooms')
G 'Gentlemen's Rooms or Lords Rooms'
H The stage
J The hanging being put up round the stage
K The 'Hell' under the stage
L The stage trap, leading down to the Hell
MM Stage doors

N Curtained 'place behind the stage'
O Gallery above the stage, used as required sometimes by musicians, sometimes by spectators, and often as part of the play
P Back-stage area (the tiring-house)
Q Tiring-house door
R Dressing-rooms
S Wardrobe and storage
T The hut housing the machine for lowering enthroned gods, etc., to the stage
U The 'Heavens'
W Hoisting the playhouse flag

down in 1613 when a cannon was fired during a performance of Shakespeare's *Henry VIII*.

With the completion in 1996 of Sam Wanamaker's project to construct in London a replica of the Globe, and with productions now running there, a version of Shakespeare's theatre can be experienced at first-hand. It is very different to the usual modern experience of drama. The form of the Elizabethan theatre derived from the inn yards and animal baiting rings in which actors had been accustomed to perform in the past. They were circular wooden buildings with a paved courtyard in the middle open to the sky. A rectangular stage jutted out into the middle of this yard. Some of the audience stood in the yard (or 'pit') to watch the play. They were thus on three sides of the stage, close up to it and on a level with it. These 'groundlings' paid only a penny to get in, but for wealthier spectators there were seats in three covered tiers or galleries between the inner and outer walls of the building, extending round most of the auditorium and overlooking the pit and the stage. Such a theatre could hold about 3,000 spectators. The yards were about 80ft in diameter and the rectangular stage approximately 40ft by 30ft and 5ft 6in high. Shakespeare aptly called such a theatre a 'wooden O' in the Prologue to *Henry V* (line 13).

The stage itself was partially covered by a roof or canopy which projected from the wall at the rear of the stage and was supported by two posts at the front. This protected the stage and performers from inclement weather, and to it were secured winches and other machinery for stage effects. On either side at the back of the stage was a door. These led into the dressing room (or 'tiring house') and it was by means of these doors that actors entered and left the stage. Between these doors was a small recess or alcove which was curtained off. Such a 'discovery place' served, for example, for Juliet's bedroom when in Act IV Scene 4 of *Romeo and Juliet* the Nurse went to the back of the stage and drew the curtain to find, or 'discover' in Elizabethan English, Juliet apparently dead on her bed. Above the discovery place was a balcony, used for the famous balcony scenes of *Romeo and Juliet* (Act II Scene 2 and Act III Scene 5), or for the battlements of Richard's castle when he is confronted by Bolingbroke in *Richard II* (Act III Scene 3). Actors (all parts in the Elizabethan theatre were taken by boys or men) had access to the area beneath the stage; from here, in the 'cellarage', would have come the voice of the ghost of Hamlet's father (*Hamlet* II.1.150–82).

On these stages there was very little in the way of scenery or props – there was nowhere to store them (there were no wings in this theatre) nor any way to set them up (no tabs across the stage), and, anyway, productions had to be transportable for performance at court or at noble houses. The stage was bare, which is why characters often tell us where they are: there was nothing on the stage to indicate location. It is also why location is so rarely topographical, and much more often symbolic. It suggests a dramatic mood or situation, rather than a place: Lear's barren heath reflects his destitute state, and the storm his emotional turmoil.

None of the plays printed in Shakespeare's lifetime marks act or scene divisions. These have been introduced by later editors, but they should not mislead us into supposing that there was any break in Elizabethan performances such as might happen today while the curtains are closed and the set is changed. The staging of Elizabethan plays was continuous, with the many short 'scenes' of which Shakespeare's plays are often constructed following one after another in quick succession. We have to think of a more fluid, and much faster, production than we are generally used to: in the prologues to *Romeo and Juliet* (line 12) and *Henry VIII* (line 13) Shakespeare speaks of only two hours as the playing time. It is because plays were staged continuously that exits and entrances are written in as part of the script: characters speak as the enter or leave the stage because otherwise there would be a silence while, in full view, they took up their positions. (This is also why dead bodies have to be carried off: they cannot get up and walk off.)

In 1608 Shakespeare's company, the King's men, acquired the Blackfriars Theatre, a smaller, rectangular indoor theatre, holding about 700 people, with seats for all the members of the audience, facilities for elaborate stage effects and, because it was enclosed, artificial lighting. It has been suggested that the plays written for this 'private' theatre differed from those written for the Globe, since, as it cost more to go to a private theatre, the audience came from a higher social stratum and demanded the more elaborate and courtly entertainment which Shakespeare's romances provide. However, the King's Men continued to play in the Globe in the summer, using Blackfriars in the winter, and it is not certain that Shakespeare's last plays were written specifically for the Blackfriars theatre, or first performed there.

Shakespeare's plays were written for this stage, but there is also a sense in which they were written *by* this stage. The material and physical circumstances of their production in such theatres had a profound effect upon the nature of Elizabethan plays. Unless we bear this in mind, we are likely to find them very strange, for we will read with expectations shaped by our own familiarity with modern fiction and modern drama. This is, by and large, realistic; it seeks to persuade us that what we are reading or watching is really happening. This is quite foreign to Shakespeare. If we try to read him like this, we shall find ourselves irritated by the improbabilities of his plot, confused by his chronology, puzzled by locations, frustrated by unanswered questions and dissatisfied by the motivation of the action. The absurd ease with which disguised persons pass through Shakespeare's plays is a case in point: why does no one recognise people they know so well? There is a great deal of psychological accuracy in Shakespeare's plays, but we are far from any attempt at realism.

The reason is that in Shakespeare's theatre it was impossible to pretend that the audience was not watching a contrived performance. In a modern theatre, the audience is encouraged to forget itself as it becomes absorbed by the action on stage. The worlds of the spectators and of the actors are sharply distinguished by the lighting: in the dark auditorium the audience is passive, silent, anonymous, receptive and attentive; on the lighted stage the actors are active, vocal, demonstrative and dramatic. (The distinction is, of course, still more marked in the cinema.) There is no communication between the two worlds: for the audience to speak would be interruptive; for the actors to address the audience would be to break the illusion of the play. In the Elizabethan theatre, this distinction did not exist, and for two reasons: first, performances took place in the open air and in daylight which illuminated every one equally; secondly, the spectators were all around the stage (and wealthier spectators actually on it), and were dressed no differently to the actors, who wore contemporary dress. In such a theatre, spectators would be as aware of each other as of the actors; they could not lose their identity in a corporate group, nor could they ever forget that they were spectators at a performance. There was no chance that they could believe 'this is really happening'.

This, then, was communal theatre, not only in the sense that it was going on in the middle of a crowd but in the sense that the crowd joined

y

in. Elizabethan audiences had none of our deference: they did not keep quiet, or arrive on time, or remain for the whole performance. They joined in, interrupted, even getting on the stage. And plays were preceded and followed by jigs and clowning. It was all much more like our experience of a pantomime, and at a pantomime we are fully aware, and are meant to be aware, that we are watching games being played with reality. The conventions of pantomime revel in their own artificiality: the fishnet tights are to signal that the handsome prince is a woman, the Dame's monstrous false breasts signal that 'she' is a man.

Something very similar is the case with Elizabethan theatre: it utilised its very theatricality. Instead of trying to persuade spectators that they are not in a theatre watching a performance, Elizabethan plays acknowledge the presence of the audience. It is addressed not only by prologues, epilogues and **choruses**, but in **soliloquies**. There is no realistic reason why characters should suddenly explain themselves to empty rooms, but, of course, it is not an empty room. The actor is surrounded by people. Soliloquies are not addressed to the world of the play; they are for the audience's benefit. And that audience's complicity is assumed: when a character like Prospero declares himself to be invisible, it is accepted that he is. Disguises are taken to be impenetrable, however improbable, and we are to accept impossibly contrived situations, such as barely hidden characters remaining undetected (indeed, on the Elizabethan stage there was nowhere at all they could hide).

These, then, are plays which are aware of themselves as dramas; in critical terminology, they are **self-reflexive**, commenting upon themselves as dramatic pieces and prompting the audience to think about the theatrical experience. They do this not only through their direct address to the audience but through their fondness for the play-within-a-play (which reminds the audience that the encompassing play is also a play) and their constant use of **images** from, and **allusions** to, the theatre. They are fascinated by role playing, by acting, appearance and reality. Things are rarely what they seem, either in **comedy** (for example, in *A Midsummer Night's Dream*) or tragedy (*Romeo and Juliet*). This offers one way to think about those disguises: they are thematic rather than realistic. Kent's disguise in *Lear* reveals his true, loyal self, while Edmund, who is not disguised, hides his true self. In *As You Like It*, Rosalind is more truly herself disguised as a man than when dressed as a woman.

The effect of all this is to confuse the distinction we would make between 'real life' and 'acting'. The case of Rosalind, for example, raises searching questions about gender roles, about how far it is 'natural' to be womanly or manly: how does the stage, on which a man can play a woman playing a man (and have a man fall in love with him/her), differ from life, in which we assume the roles we think appropriate to masculine and feminine behaviour? The same is true of political roles: when a Richard II or Lear is so aware of the regal part he is performing, of the trappings and rituals of kingship, their plays raise the uncomfortable possibility that the answer to the question, what constitutes a successful king, is simply: a good actor. Indeed, human life generally is repeatedly rendered through the imagery of the stage, from Macbeth's 'Life's but a walking shadow, a poor player/ That struts and frets his hour upon the stage/ And then is heard no more ...' (V.5.23–5) to Prospero's paralleling of human life to a performance which, like the globe (both world and theatre) will end (*The Tempest* IV.I.146–58). When life is a fiction, like this play, or this play is a fiction like life, what is the difference? 'All the world's a stage ...' (*As You Like It* II.7.139).

THEATRICAL AND LITERARY BACKGROUND

We can be reasonably sure that *Henry IV Part I* was written and first performed in London around late 1596 or early 1597. Shakespeare had already written his four plays on the Wars of the Roses which followed the death of King Henry V (the Prince Hal of *1* and *Henry IV Part II*), and the play dealing with the usurpation of Richard II's throne by Hal's father, Henry Bolingbroke (*Richard II*). As might be guessed from their subject matter, the tone of these plays is predominantly serious (indeed, *Richard II* was known in its time as a tragedy). In *Henry IV Part I* Shakespeare made his first sustained attempt to mingle comic and serious material in a historical play, and in doing so experimented with aspects of dramatic genre already explored by other companies and writers.

The English history play first appeared on stage in the 1580s, a period during which several pressing political problems focused attention on the lessons to be learnt from the past. Protestant England had existed uneasily with the great powers of Catholic Europe since Elizabeth I's coming to the throne in 1558, but by the 1580s the situation had degenerated into open hostility. In 1579, an Irish revolt against English rule had been blessed by the Pope; in 1581 the English began hunting down and executing Catholic priests for treason, and in 1585 Elizabeth sent troops to support Protestants fighting in the Low Countries against their Catholic Spanish rulers. In 1587, the Catholic Scottish Queen Mary Stuart was executed for conspiring to overthrow Elizabeth, and in 1588 the Spanish Armada was sent against England.

The patriotism engendered by such a political climate led to a demand for historical plays, particularly when they were patriotic or dealt with English victories. More generally, history was continually searched for the lessons it could teach the present. Two of the earliest history plays, both from the 1580s, focused on the reigns of King John (supposedly poisoned by a Catholic monk for his defiance of the Pope) and Henry V. The titles – *The Troublesome Reign of King John* and *The Famous Victories of Henry V* – show the ways in which plays on historical subject matter could both celebrate the past and question it for its contemporary relevance.

These two plays came out of a theatre which relied heavily on the skills of actors. Indeed, it is often suggested that the texts of these plays were in some part put together by actors. Though they use iambic pentameter, they make little attempt to aim at poetic language. But by the time Shakespeare came to write his history plays, Christopher Marlowe's *Tamburlaine, Edward II*, and *The Massacre at Paris* had shown how plays with historical subject matter could incorporate the poetic verse pioneered by the university wits of the late 1580s. To generalise, the theatre during the 1590s relied more on the skills of the writers and less on the skills of the actors than it had in the 1580s.

The theatre of the 1590s relied on writers in another important way. In the early years of purpose-built theatres in London, theatre companies made their living from touring the provinces. They might only pass through a town once a year, and so needed to update their repertoire relatively infrequently. But once the same companies were based for at least part of the year in London, they had to keep coming up with new material, to hold onto their audience and to compete with other companies. Once it became clear that historical plays would hold an audience, companies invested heavily in them, producing rival versions of the same events, and turning out sequels (and, sometimes, prequels) to popular plays. We know, for example, that in 1595 and 1596, just before Shakespeare wrote *Henry IV Part I*, a rival company put on a play called 'Harry the fifth' in London. This may well have been a version of *The Famous Victories of Henry the Fifth*, which, though dealing largely with Henry V's victory at Agincourt, also devotes some space to his life as prince Hal before he became king.

Shakespeare almost never invented the plots for his plays. But in the case of *Henry IV Part I* he probably went one further, and used as his starting point another company's play, *The Famous Victories*. As was usual when he was writing his historical plays, he read around the subject, certainly consulting Raphael Holinshed's *Chronicles* (1587) and possibly other historical works. He also looked at a recently published long historical poem, Samuel Daniel's *First Four Books of the Civil Wars* (1595). Along with minor suggestions of emphasis, he took from Daniel's poem the idea of making Hotspur and Prince Hal the same age, and of having them meet in combat (in fact, Hotspur was older than King Henry, Hal's father). But he also took some suggestions from *The Famous Victories of Henry V*. Elements Shakespeare used in *Henry IV Part I* include a tavern at Eastcheap, the prince's participation in a robbery, his defence of another thief friend of his against the forces of law and order, a play-acting scene in which two commoners play the prince and the lord chief justice, and the king's complaints about his wayward son. It also features three companions for the prince, Ned, Tom, and Sir John Oldcastle. The latter name belonged to a real historical character, who was executed for heresy and treason in the reign of Henry V.

The Famous Victories is only a starting point for some elements of *Henry IV Part I*. But its use of Sir John Oldcastle had consequences for Shakespeare's play, for it is now generally agreed that the original name for Falstaff was Oldcastle, and that this was changed as the result of political pressure from Oldcastle's descendants. The original Oldcastle's heresy was a doctrine close to Protestantism, and he was considered a martyr by many after the Reformation. Falstaff, of course, uses religious language a great deal, though in a spirit of mockery. Whether Shakespeare's original version was intended as a snub to Oldcastle's descendants, or to pious Protestants, or simply following *The Famous Victories'* lead, he was forced to change the name, and inserted at the end of *Henry IV Part II* an **epilogue**, in which Falstaff directly states that Oldcastle was a martyr, and he is not intended to be him. Peto and Bardolph similarly are substitutions for the names Russell and Harvey.

The name change, though it seems to have prevented Shakespeare and his company getting into trouble, did not stop Falstaff from being referred to as Oldcastle in the decades immediately following, which indicates that at least in some performances this name was used. A rival company put on a play in 1599 called *Sir John Oldcastle* to put the record straight, and pulled off the coup of securing the services of the actor who probably played Falstaff, Will Kemp, for their own play. Kemp, who left Shakespeare's company between *Henry IV Part II* and *Henry V*, played an old roguish priest, cheekily called Sir John.

PART SIX

CRITICAL HISTORY AND FURTHER PERSPECTIVES

RECEPTION AND EARLY CRITICAL VIEWS

For a century and a half after the Oldcastle affair (see Background: Theatrical and Literary background), Falstaff continued to dominate accounts of, and responses to, *Henry IV Part I*. The play seems to have made an instant impact, going through two quarto editions in 1598, the year of its first publication, and a further five (in 1599, 1604, 1608, 1613, and 1622) before the publication in 1623 of the play in Shakespeare's First Folio. The first recorded quotation from the play, which uses Falstaff's words on honour, makes a sarcastic point about British military commanders in the Low Countries, and dates from as early as September 1598. More references to Falstaff survive from the seventeenth century than for any other dramatic character, and such critical discussion of *Henry IV Part I* as there is in the seventeenth and eighteenth centuries focuses largely on the fat knight.

The terms of these early critical debates are indicated by Nicholas Rowe's remark in the preface to his 1709 edition of Shakespeare that Falstaff is 'almost too agreeable', given the extent of his moral vices. The most famous character in *Henry IV Part I* is judged for his usefulness as a moral example, and found wanting. The same point was addressed with less uncertainty in 1765 by Samuel Johnson, who, whilst noting that Sir John 'is a character loaded with faults, and with those faults which naturally produce contempt', allowed him too 'the most pleasing of all qualities, perpetual gaiety ... an unfailing power of exciting laughter' (Hunter, 1970, pp. 23–4). For Johnson, however, Falstaff's comic appeal simply functions as a warning against the kind of person most dangerous to one's moral health: 'he that with a will to corrupt, hath a power to please' (Hunter, 1970, p. 24).

Given the then-dominant critical assumption that plays, and indeed all imaginative productions, should be judged for their **didactic** usefulness, it is not surprising that the first serious attempt to defend Falstaff argued

Y

that his character had been misread, and that he is in fact a model of a certain kind of 'Courage and Military Character'. Maurice Morgann's *An Essay on the Dramatic Character of Falstaff* (1777) begins from the paradox that 'we all like Old Jack; yet, by some strange perverse fate, we all abuse him, and deny him the possession of any one single good or respectable quality' (Hunter, 1970, p. 29). For Morgann, enjoyment of Falstaff is a response to genuinely admirable qualities, such as courage, which are obscured by his more showy deficiencies: 'his ill habits, and the accidents of age and corpulence, are no part of his essential constitution; they come forward indeed on our eye, and solicit our notice, but they are second natures, not first' (Hunter, 1970, p. 53). Morgann's thesis soon attracted refutations; Falstaff's wounding of the dead Hotspur was held to be a particularly cowardly act.

Nineteenth-century critics, whilst remaining interested in Falstaff, also began to take more of an interest in other characters, particularly Hotspur and Hal. As eighteenth-century Gothic metamorphosed into Victorian medievalism, critics began to focus not merely on characters' morality, but on their exemplifying a nostalgic sense of the values of a medieval world at odds with the 'modern' nineteenth century. Critics began to read the plays with expectations formed by Walter Scott's medieval romances' focus on chivalry and honour. Both Hal and Hotspur, the prime embodiments of these virtues, were often seen virtually uncritically as chivalric heroes. For example, the influential German critic August Wilhelm Schlegel wrote in 1808 in his *Lectures on Dramatic Art and Literature* (translated into English in 1815) that though Falstaff is 'the crown of Shakespeare's comic invention', the play

> is particularly brilliant in the serious scenes, from the contrast between the two young heroes, Prince Henry and Percy (with the characteristical name of Hotspur). All the amiability and attractiveness is certainly on the side of the prince: however familiar he makes himself with bad company, can never mistake him for one of them: the ignoble does indeed touch, but it does not contaminate him; and his wildest freaks appear merely as witty tricks, by which his restless mind sought to burst through the inactivity to which he was constrained, for on the first occasion which wakes him out of his unruly levity he distinguishes himself without effort in the most chivalrous guise. Percy's boisterous valour is not without a mixture of rude manners, arrogance, and boyish obstinacy; but these errors, which prepare him for an early death, cannot

disfigure the majestic image of his noble youth; we are carried away by his fiery spirit at the very moment we would most censure it. (Bate, 1992, pp. 353–4)

Perhaps the clearest indication of this change of emphasis in critical approach is seen in the words of William Hazlitt, an admirer of Schlegel, who wrote in 1817 in his *Characters of Shakespeare's Plays* that 'the heroic and serious part of these two founded on the story of Henry IV is not inferior to the comic and farcical. The characters of Hotspur and Prince Henry are two of the most beautiful and dramatic, both in themselves and from contrast, that were ever drawn. They are the essence of chivalry' (Bate, 1992, pp. 359–60).

Jonathan Bate, (ed), *The Romantics on Shakespeare*, Penguin, 1992
> This anthology includes extracts from Hazlitt, Inchbald and Schlegel on the play, as well as a range of other commentary on Shakespeare's historical plays

G K Hunter, (ed), *King Henry IV Parts 1 & 2*, Macmillan, 1970
> This anthology of criticism includes extracts from Johnson and Morgann, as well as Bradley, Dover Wilson, Tillyard, and Barber (referred to in the next section)

Ronald Knowles, *Henry IV Parts I & II*, Macmillan, 1992
> This is a thorough introduction to the variety of criticism on both plays from the earliest days to the 1990s. It intelligently discusses most of the critics referred to in this chapter, and also includes an original appraisal of the play by Knowles

Brian Vickers, (ed), *William Shakespeare: The Critical Heritage*, 6 volumes, Routledge, 1974
> This collects responses to and criticism of Shakespeare's works, on both page and stage, from the earliest period to the nineteenth century

THE TWENTIETH CENTURY

The twentieth century opened with one of the greatest Shakespearean character critics shifting the terms of critical debate on the play. A.C. Bradley, already the author of the most influential book of Shakespeare criticism of his era (*Shakespearean Tragedy*, 1904) published an essay on 'The Rejection of Falstaff' in his *Oxford Lectures on Poetry* (1909) in which he turned again to the relationship between Hal and Falstaff, reading it in the light of the prince's rejection of the latter once he becomes king at the end of *Henry IV Part II*. Bradley repudiates the eighteenth-century moral approach to character study, stating that Falstaff is 'a character almost purely humorous, and therefore no subject for moral judgements' (Bradley, 1909, p. 260). Like Morgann's defence of Falstaff, Bradley's could be accused of idealisation, for example in its over-ingenious interpretation of Falstaff's cowardice ('when he saw Henry and Hotspur fighting, Falstaff, instead of making off in a panic, stayed to take his chance if Hotspur should be the victor,' p. 267). Falstaff stands for something greater than himself: 'the bliss of freedom gained in humour is the essence of Falstaff' (p. 262).

Bradley's insistence on treating Falstaff as if he were a real person, which goes as far as to construct a basic chronology of his life from the two *Henry IV* plays, was answered by a counter-movement in early-twentieth-century criticism attacking the very idea of character criticism itself. Critics such as E.E. Stoll, John Dover Wilson, and, most influentially, E.M.W. Tillyard, read the play through theatre history, insisting that when they were written audiences did not expect the kind of 'three-dimensional' characters in which the novel was later to specialise. European theatre from the classical period to the Renaissance relied heavily on what we would now call **types**, (or, in everyday language, stereotypes) such as the clown, the young lover, the miserly old man or the boastful soldier (**miles gloriosus**). Stoll insisted that an audience used to such stock roles would have slotted Falstaff into them without a second thought. Boastful soldiers were cowards, so Falstaff would be seen as a coward at Shrewsbury rather than somebody *pretending* to be one, as Morgann and Bradley attempted to argue. Wilson and Tillyard went further, claiming that the sixteenth-century **morality play**, which dealt almost exclusively in such types, and which lasted in the theatres up until the time Shakespeare began writing, would have accustomed audiences to quick judgements of characters along orthodox moral or political lines. The aim of the morality play was to teach its audience how to avoid vice and embrace virtue (often in explicitly Christian terms), and a typical moral play would feature a variety of types of virtue and vice. The dramatis personae of the late morality play *Like Will to Like* (1589) gives a reasonable sense of the degree to which these could be seen as 'characters', featuring as it does Vertuous Life, God's Promise, Honour, Good Fame, Rafe Roister, Tom Tospot, and Cutbert Cutpurse.

The plot of a morality play centres around the choice between good and bad, and makes every effort (as the names above suggest) to ensure an audience is not misled into believing that Tom Tospot is preferable to Vertuous Life. Reading *Henry IV Part I* through the morality play thus requires that characters be slotted into 'good' or 'bad' roles, and led Tillyard into this kind of abstract account of the play:

> In the first part the Prince (who, one knows, will soon be king) is tested in the military or chivalric virtues. He has to choose, Morality-fashion, between Sloth or Vanity, to which he is drawn by his bad companions, and Chivalry, to which he is drawn by his father and his brothers. And he chooses Chivalry. The action is complicated by Hotspur and Falstaff, who stand for the excess and the defect of the military spirit, for honour exaggerated and dishonour. Thus the Prince, as well as being [a character] in a Morality Play, is Aristotle's middle quality between two extremes. (Tillyard, 1986, pp. 270–1)

Falstaff and Hotspur are thus reduced to 'examples' to be avoided, and Hal raised to be the hero of the play. Tillyard compares him favourably with Hotspur, as a refined courtier in contrast to Hotspur, who 'verges on the ridiculous from the very beginning, through his childish inability to control his passions' (p. 288). Falstaff stands for Misrule or Disorder, and, as such, has been sentimentalised by those such as Bradley who saw him as a symbol of freedom. Tillyard, writing in the middle of the Second World War, unsurprisingly valued order above all:

> The school of criticism that furnished him with a tender heart and condemned the Prince for brutality in turning him away was deluded. Its delusion will probably be accounted for, in later years, through the facts of history. The sense of security created in nineteenth-century England by the predominance of the British navy induced men to rate that very security too cheaply and to exalt the instinct of rebellion above its legitimate station. They forgot the threat of disorder which was ever present with the Elizabethans. Schooled by recent events we should have no difficulty now in taking Falstaff as the Elizabethans took him. (Tillyard, 1986, p. 296)

Tillyard's work was very influential for some decades, and much criticism of the play tended to see it as, broadly, Hal's play rather than Falstaff's or Hotspur's, and to focus on its political orthodoxy.

A.C. Bradley, *Oxford Lectures on Poetry*, Macmillan, 1909

A.C. Bradley, *Shakespearean Tragedy*, Macmillan, 1904

E.E. Stoll, *Shakespeare Studies*, New York, 1927

E.M.W. Tillyard, *Shakespeare's History Plays*, Chatto and Windus, 1944, reprinted in Pelican, 1986 (references are to this edition)

John Dover Wilson, *The Fortunes of Falstaff*, Cambridge University Press, 1943

RECENT APPROACHES

Since the 1960s, Tillyard's interpretation of the play has been challenged on many fronts. Broadly speaking, recent critics are less inclined to see the play as orthodox in its presentation of politics, and are less likely to see characters as unified wholes. Resistance to Tillyard is rooted in a wide range of critical approaches, from Robert Ornstein's insistence in *A Kingdom For A Stage* (Harvard University Press, 1972) that a great writer like Shakespeare is unlikely to have written a play as simplistic as Tillyard's account makes it seem, to a range of critics informed by developments in literary theory.

FEMINISM

Elizabeth Inchbald wrote in 1808 of *Henry IV Part I* that it is 'a play which all men admire and most women dislike' (Bate, 1992, p. 353). Feminist critics in the 1960s and 1970s tended not to write on history plays, preferring to focus on other plays with more prominent female roles. More recently, critics have approached the play from a variety of feminist viewpoints, drawing on psychoanalytic theory, cultural materialism and performance history.

Though the female characters in the play have relatively small roles, they share some characteristics. There are no women at Henry IV's court. They are present only at the margins of the play – Wales, Eastcheap, Percy's base in the north. When they do appear, women are presented as in some way or other deviating from a male 'norm' of behaviour. They speak differently to men. Mistress Quickly has her malapropisms and misunderstandings, Mortimer's wife speaks and sings entirely in Welsh. They are demonstrative with their emotions, particularly affection. They are associated with idleness and leisure. They do not accept their exclusion from the 'real', public world: both Lady Percy and Mortimer's wife try to accompany their husbands to war. Though women are marginal characters in the play, they disrupt, or threaten to disrupt, the smooth running of the (men only) plot.

As might be expected in a play dealing with both war and becoming a man, how masculinity is constituted is one of the play's main themes. But being a man is not merely doing masculine things and thinking masculine thoughts. It also involves avoiding their opposite, the feminine. Hotspur in particular frequently attacks effeminacy. Examples include his description of the courtier on the battlefield, perfumed, recoiling at nasty smells and sights, his insistence to Lady Percy that 'This is no world/ To play with mammets, and to tilt with lips' (II.3. 94–5), and his rejection with Glendower of 'mincing poetry'. Hal's relationship with the feminine is different, and centres around Falstaff. Though he is not effeminate, Falstaff is not properly masculine either. He is not brave, straightforward, or honest; he is cowardly on the battlefield, and at Gad's Hill, mocks 'honour', and claims credit for things he has not done. Falstaff clearly does not care about honour; but this means he does not care for a certain kind of masculinity, and offers Hal the option of a gender identity not effeminate, but not masculine in Hotspur's terms either.

Peter Erickson, *Patriarchal Structures in Shakespeare's Drama*, California University Press, Berkeley and London, 1985

Barbara Hodgdon, *The End Crowns All*, Princeton University Press, 1991

Jean Howard and Phyllis Rackin, *Engendering a Nation*, Routledge, 1997

Coppelia Kahn, *Man's Estate: Masculine Identity in Shakespeare*, California University Press, Berkeley and London, 1981

PSYCHOANALYSIS

Psychoanalytic approaches to the play revisit some of the key areas of debate regarding the play, whilst providing a fresh approach to them. Hal remains central to psychoanalytic readings. In contrast to earlier critics, who saw no real change in his character during the play, these critics read the play as centrally concerned with the process of his growing up, and throughout the play as a whole the problems for sons of inadequate fathers and for fathers of inadequate sons. It also provides both a defence of Falstaff against charges of immorality, and an explanation for the prince's ambivalent relationship with him.

Many psychoanalytic critics are also feminists, but some areas of psychoanalytic criticism of the play do not have distinctively feminist overtones. Psychoanalytic criticism often focuses on character, but reads it in the light of Freudian and post-Freudian theories of the psyche. Central to these is the insistence on the importance of the conventional heterosexual family unit in the development of the individual, and the relations between the individual and maternal and paternal influences. For men, the usual process of development into maturity begins with aggression toward both father and mother, the mother because of her power over the infant, and the father because he threatens the relationship between mother and child. As he matures,the infant must work through his ambivalence towards an acceptance of his father (the **Oedipus complex**) and rejection of his mother.

Henry IV Part I is full of the problematic relationships between actual and metaphorical fathers and sons. Hal's family unit has no women; rather it encompasses difficult relations with his father, who lacks legitimate authority, as he has usurped the throne, and with Falstaff, with whom there is a similar tension between acceptance and repudiation. Similarly, from the king's perspective, his son at the play's beginning commands no respect, and indeed he wishes he could exchange him for Hotspur.

Hotspur himself has two inadequate father-figures, Worcester and Northumberland, for whom he is a frustrating 'son', whose advice he is unable to listen to, and who eventually betray him to save themselves. Despite its public focus, then, the drama is driven by familial or quasi-familial relationships

Standing on your own feet as a man, as feminist critics have noted in regard to Mortimer and Hotspur, involves a negotiation with, and often a rejection of, the actual and metaphorical feminine. The exception to this is in Hal's relationship to England, which is gendered feminine by the king at the very beginning of the play. Civil war is imagined as wounding the mother country ('No more the thirsty entrance of this soil/ Shall daub her lips with her own children's blood', I.1.5–6) and the crusade Henry proposes will be undertaken by soldiers 'Whose arms were moulded in their mother's womb' (I.1.23). Henry must take the blame for this initial state of affairs, as his usurpation of Richard II's throne is its root cause. Though he seeks to purge what is in effect a crime against a symbolic mother by offering penance and crusade, he is unable to wipe out the damage he has done.

Other male characters can be read as reaching different stages in the process of maturation Hal is going through. Psychoanalysis recognises that this is neither an inevitable nor a painless process, but insists that it must be confronted, and that avoiding or repressing it is more destructive in the long run. As Richard Wheeler notes in his book *Shakespeare's Development and the Problem Comedies* (1981), 'Glendower's aspiration to magical omnipotence, Hotspur's narcissistic pursuit of self-idealization through honor, Falstaff's gluttony for a world of timeless sensual satiation' (p. 164) characterise them as to a greater or lesser degree infantile. Falstaff is a more complex figure than the other two in regard to Hal's development, as he also functions as father-figure, nurturer, and companion in playfulness. Because Hal is able to recognise his own needs, in the safe space of Eastcheap, and under Falstaff's supervision, he is able to avoid projecting them into the public arena. Private play, including imitating both his own father and his father-figure in the crucial scene Act 2 Scene 4, enables him to grow up in public. Because Hal has, in this sense, two fathers, he can both reject and accept paternal authority.

Barbara Hodgdon, *The End Crowns All*, Princeton University Press, 1991

Jean Howard and Phyllis Rackin, *Engendering a Nation*, Routledge, 1997

Coppelia Kahn, *Man's Estate: Masculine Identity in Shakespeare*, California University Press, Berkeley and London, 1981

Valerie Traub, *Desire and Anxiety*, Routledge, 1992

Richard Wheeler, *Shakespeare's Development and the Problem Comedies*, California University Press, Berkeley and London, 1981

NEW HISTORICISM AND CULTURAL MATERIALISM

Criticism of *Henry IV Part I* has always worked with a theory, implicit or explicit, of how power (especially political power) operates. One of the accounts of the play most influential in the move away from Tillyard-centred reading of the play's politics has been C.L. Barber's chapter in his *Shakespeare's Festive Comedy* (1959). Barber sees the comic in Shakespeare functioning in the same way as various rituals and folk customs did in Renaissance England – to provide a release from the oppressiveness of the everyday, after which the individual is better able to function again within society. In the two *Henry IV* plays, 'Shakespeare dramatizes not only holiday but also the need for holiday and the need to limit holiday' (p. 192). Barber represents Falstaff and the Eastcheap world as diversions from, rather than serious alternatives to, the world of responsibility and high politics. In Hal's words, 'If all the year were playing holidays,/ To sport would be as tedious as to work' (I.2.202–3). Even Falstaff's intelligently satirical commentary is repudiated at the play's end, as Hal successfully enters the public world of honour. Honour is more than 'a word', but the play's recognition that there is a counterview simply works to strengthen its final conclusion.

Barber's consideration of the relationship between the play's comic elements and political power was addressed in 'Invisible Bullets', an extremely influential article by Stephen Greenblatt (1992), and something of a manifesto for the New Historicist critical approach to Shakespeare's plays. Greenblatt's agrees that Hal is 'an ideal image' of a ruler-in-waiting, but explores the idea that 'such an ideal image involves as its positive condition the constant production of its own radical subversion and the powerful containment of that subversion' (p. 94). Beginning from Hal's declared intent in Act 1 Scene 2 to manipulate his life in Eastcheap for his own purposes, Greenblatt suggests that the opposition between Eastcheap and the court, noted by Barber, is actively produced by the prince himself, and that such 'holiday' (or, in Greenblatt's terms, subversive) elements as there are are set up by Hal and under his control. Not only is the play-world of Eastcheap never a threat to Hal, but his mastery of it depends upon his mastery of play itself. This is indicated in miniature in his treatment of Francis the drawer in Act II Scene 4, where he both suggests he rebel against the indignities of his job and humiliates him. His ability to

adopt different roles depending on the situation is the prerequisite for his
success:

> Hal's characteristic activity is playing or, more precisely, theatrical improvisation – his
> parts include his father, Hotspur, Hotspur's wife, a thief in buckram, himself as
> prodigal and himself as penitent – and he fully understands his own behaviour
> through most of the play as a role that he is performing. (Greenblatt, 1992, p. 97)

Graham Holderness in *Shakespeare Recycled* (1992) argues against
Greenblatt (and, through him, with the critical tradition stretching back
through Barber at least to Tillyard and Dover Wilson which sees Falstaff
as subordinate to the main action of the play) by insisting on the
differences between Falstaff's world and that of the nobles. This plebeian
holiday world is opposed to aristocratic 'normality' not merely in the sense
that it is juxtaposed with it in the play, but also because it is hostile to it.
The fact that things do not turn out the way Falstaff might want them to
does not negate the power of what Holderness calls his 'utopian
anarchism'. This is not so much a practical programme as a 'political
discourse uncompromising in its extremity of demand for freedom, peace,
justice and plenty' (p. 160). He gives as an example Falstaff's 'shall there be
gallows standing in England when thou art King?' (I.25.8–9), noting that
'this image of a society without punishment is a vigorous and beautiful
dream of human aspiration' (p. 160).

C.L. Barber, *Shakespeare's Festive Comedy*, Princeton University Press, 1959

Stephen Greenblatt, 'Invisible Bullets: Renaissance Authority and its
Subversion, *Henry IV* and *Henry V*', reprinted in Richard Wilson and
Richard Dutton (eds), *New Historicism and Renaissance Drama*, Longman,
1992

Graham Holderness, *Shakespeare Recycled*, Harvester, 1992

Kiernan Ryan, *Shakespeare* (2nd edition), Harvester, 1995

OTHER STUDIES

Harry Berger, Jr., *Making Trifles of Terrors*, Stanford University Press, 1997

This collection of essays contains an up to date and theoretically aware consideration of 'Hotspur and honor'

Graham Holderness (ed), *Shakespeare's History Plays: Richard II to Henry V*, Macmillan, 1992

A collection of some of the most influential recent readings of Shakespeare's major histories

Graham Holderness, *Shakespeare: The Histories*, Macmillan, 2000

The essay on *Henry IV Part I* in this collection considers the processes of history– and myth-making in the play

Scott McMillin, *Henry IV, Part One*, Manchester University Press, 1991

McMillin traces the history of the play on the stage, with general material and detailed accounts of specific productions

Robert Ornstein, *A Kingdom For A Stage*, Cambridge, MA: Harvard University Press, 1972

Traditional criticism, paying close attention to the text, with the aim of rescuing Shakespeare from the role of Tudor propagandist

David Wiles, *Shakespeare's Clown*, Cambridge University Press, 1987

This book traces the figure of the clown on the Elizabethan stage, showing how Falstaff is rooted in traditions of popular entertainment

World events	Shakespeare's life	Literary events
1492 Columbus sails to America		
		1513 Niccolò Machiavelli, *The Prince*
1534 Henry VIII breaks with Rome and declares himself head of the Church of England		
1556 Archbishop Cranmer burnt at the stake		
1558 Elizabeth I accedes to throne		
	1564 Born in Stratford-upon-Avon	
		1565 Giambattisa Cinzio Giraldi, *The Hecatommithi*
		1565-7 English translation, by Arthur Golding, of Ovid's *Metamorphosis*
1568 Mary Queen of Scots taken prisoner by Elizabeth I		
1570 Elizabeth I excommunicated by Pope Pius V		
1571 The Battle of Lepanto		
		1576 Erection of the first specially built public theatres in London - the Theatre and the Curtain
1577 Francis Drake sets out on round the world voyage		
1579 Irish revolt against English rule is blessed by the Pope		
1581 Catholic priests are accused of treason		**1581** Barnabe Rich, *Farewell to Military Profession*
1582 Outbreak of the Plague in London	**1582** Marries Anne Hathaway	

y

World events	Shakespeare's life	Literary events
	1583 His daughter, Susanna, is born	
1584 Raleigh's sailors land in Virginia		**1584** French translation, by Gabriel Chappuys, of Cinzio's *The Hecatommithi*
	1585 His twins, Hamnet and Judith, born	
	c1585-92 Moves to London	
	late 1580s-early 90s Probably writes *Henry VI (Parts I, II, III)* and *Richard III*	
1586 Elizabeth sends troops to support Protestants fighting in the Low Country against Catholic Spain		
1587 Execution of Mary Queen of Scots after implication in plot to murder Elizabeth I		**1587** Christopher Marlowe, *Tamburlaine the Great;* Raphael Holinshed, *Chronicles*
1588 The Spanish Armada defeated		
1589 Accession of Henri IV to French throne		**1589** (c) Kyd, *The Spanish Tragedy* (first revenge tragedy)
		1590 Spenser, *The Faerie Queene*
1592 Plague in London closes theatres	**1592** Writes *The Comedy of Errors*	**1592** Marlowe, *Doctor Faustus*
	1593 Writes *Titus Andronicus, The Taming of the Shrew*	
	1594 onwards Writes exclusively for the Lord Chamberlain's Men; writes *Two Gentlemen of Verona, Love's Labours Lost, Richard II*	

World events	Shakespeare's life	Literary events
	1595 Writes *Romeo and Juliet, A Midsummer Night's Dream*	**1595** Samuel Daniel, *First Four Books of the Civil Wars*
1596 Drake perishes on expedition to West Indies	**1596** Hamnet dies; William granted coat of arms; *Henry IV (Parts I and II)* written	
	1598 Writes *Much Ado About Nothing*	**1598** Christopher Marlowe, *Hero and Leander*
	1599 Buys share in the Globe Theatre; writes *Julius Caesar, As You Like It, Twelfth Night; Henry V* completed	
	1600 *The Merchant of Venice* printed	**1600** John Parry, *History and Description of Africa*
	1600-1 Writes *Hamlet, The Merry Wives of Windsor*	
	1601 Writes *Troilus and Cressida*	
	1602 Writes *All's Well That Ends Well*	
	1602-4 Probably writes *Othello*	
1603 Death of Queen Elizabeth I; accession of James I	**1603 onwards** His company enjoys patronage of James I as The King's Men	**1603** Marston's *The Malcontent* first performed
	1604 *Othello* performed; writes *Measure for Measure*	
1605 Discovery of Guy Fawkes's plot to blow up the Houses of Parliament	**1605** First version of *King Lear*	**1605** Cervantes, *Don Quijote de la Mancha*

y

World events	Shakespeare's life	Literary events
	1606 Writes *Macbeth*	
	1606-7 Probably writes *Antony and Cleopatra*	
	1607 Writes *Coriolanus, Timon of Athens*	**1607** Tourneur's *The Revenger's Tragedy* published
	1608 Writes *Pericles.* The King's Men acquire Blackfriars Theatre for winter performances	
1609 Galileo constructs first astronomical telescope	**1609** Becomes part-owner of the new Blackfriars Theatre	
1610 Henri IV of France assassinated William Harvey discovers circulation of blood; Galileo observes Saturn for the first time		
	1611 *Cymbeline, The Winter's Tale* and *The Tempest* performed	**1611** King James's translation of the Bible
1612 Last burning of heretics in England	**1612** Shakespeare retires from London theatre and returns to Stratford	**1612** Webster, *The White Devil*
	1613 The Globe Theatre burns down	**1613** Webster, *Duchess of Malfi*
	1616 Dies	
1618 Raleigh executed for treason Thirty Years War begins	in England	
		1622 Birth of French dramatist Molière
	1623 *The First Folio* published	

allusion a passing reference in a work to something outside itself

blank verse unrhymed iambic pentameter

chorus an onstage narrator, sometimes adopting the position of bystander to the action

comedy a genre distinguished by an entertaining or upbeat tone and a happy ending

conceit an extended or developed image, often surprising or paradoxical

didactic intended to teach or persuade

dramatic irony the phenomenon whereby the audience knows more about the action than some or all of the characters on stage

epilogue concluding speech or passage

eulogy a formal speech praising a person who has just died

folio a large page size, formed by folding a sheet of printer's paper once

genre a kind or type of writing. Poetry, drama and the novel are genres, as are comedy and tragedy

iambic pentameter a verse line of ten syllables, with the stress falling on every second syllable

imagery a visual picture in words

in medias res (Latin) into or in the middle of things

irony saying one thing whilst meaning another

miles gloriosus (Latin) boastful soldier; a stock literary type

morality play a didactic play focusing on teaching a moral or spiritual lesson

Oedipus complex an adult male's infantile sexual desire for his mother

Quarto the size of a piece of printer's paper that has been folded four times

realist an artist or writer who seeks to represent the familiar or typical in real life rather than an idealised, formalised or romantic interpretation

self-reflexive referring to itself

soliloquy a solo dramatic speech, often but not always abiding by the convention that the audience is overhearing rather than having the speech directly addressed to them

subplot a subsidiary plot or action running alongside a main plot

tragedy a genre broadly distinguished by its ending (often the death of a main character) which deals with the fall of an often notable individual

type a character representing a group or class; a stock character

AUTHOR OF THIS NOTE

Stephen Longstaffe is Lecturer in English and Drama at St Martin's College, Lancaster, and was educated at Lancaster and York universities. His main academic interest is the Elizabethan history play.

York Notes Advanced

Margaret Atwood
Cat's Eye

Margaret Atwood
The Handmaid's Tale

Jane Austen
Emma

Jane Austen
Mansfield Park

Jane Austen
Persuasion

Jane Austen
Pride and Prejudice

Jane Austen
Sense and Sensibility

Alan Bennett
Talking Heads

William Blake
Songs of Innocence and of Experience

Charlotte Brontë
Jane Eyre

Charlotte Brontë
Villette

Emily Brontë
Wuthering Heights

Angela Carter
Nights at the Circus

Geoffrey Chaucer
The Franklin's Prologue and Tale

Geoffrey Chaucer
The Miller's Prologue and Tale

Geoffrey Chaucer
Prologue to the Canterbury Tales

Geoffrey Chaucer
The Wife of Bath's Prologue and Tale

Samuel Taylor Coleridge
Selected Poems

Joseph Conrad
Heart of Darkness

Daniel Defoe
Moll Flanders

Charles Dickens
Bleak House

Charles Dickens
Great Expectations

Charles Dickens
Hard Times

Emily Dickinson
Selected Poems

John Donne
Selected Poems

Carol Ann Duffy
Selected Poems

George Eliot
Middlemarch

George Eliot
The Mill on the Floss

T.S. Eliot
Selected Poems

T.S. Eliot
The Waste Land

F. Scott Fitzgerald
The Great Gatsby

E.M. Forster
A Passage to India

Brian Friel
Translations

Thomas Hardy
Jude the Obscure

Thomas Hardy
The Mayor of Casterbridge

Thomas Hardy
The Return of the Native

Thomas Hardy
Selected Poems

Thomas Hardy
Tess of the d'Urbervilles

Seamus Heaney
Selected Poems from Opened Ground

Nathaniel Hawthorne
The Scarlet Letter

Homer
The Iliad

Homer
The Odyssey

Aldous Huxley
Brave New World

Kazuo Ishiguro
The Remains of the Day

Ben Jonson
The Alchemist

James Joyce
Dubliners

John Keats
Selected Poems

Christopher Marlowe
Doctor Faustus

Christopher Marlowe
Edward II

Arthur Miller
Death of a Salesman

John Milton
Paradise Lost Books I & II

Toni Morrison
Beloved

George Orwell
Nineteen-Eighty-Four

Sylvia Plath
Selected Poems

Alexander Pope
Rape of the Lock and other poems

William Shakespeare
Antony and Cleopatra

William Shakespeare
As You Like It

William Shakespeare
Hamlet

William Shakespeare
King Lear

William Shakespeare
Macbeth

William Shakespeare
Measure for Measure

William Shakespeare
The Merchant of Venice

William Shakespeare
A Midsummer Night's Dream

William Shakespeare
Much Ado About Nothing

William Shakespeare
Othello

William Shakespeare
Richard II

William Shakespeare
Richard III

William Shakespeare
Romeo and Juliet

William Shakespeare
The Taming of the Shrew

William Shakespeare
The Tempest

William Shakespeare
Twelfth Night

William Shakespeare
The Winter's Tale

George Bernard Shaw
Saint Joan

Mary Shelley
Frankenstein

Jonathan Swift
Gulliver's Travels and A Modest Proposal

Alfred, Lord Tennyson
Selected Poems

Virgil
The Aeneid

Alice Walker
The Color Purple

Oscar Wilde
The Importance of Being Earnest

Tennessee Williams
A Streetcar Named Desire

Jeanette Winterson
Oranges Are Not the Only Fruit

John Webster
The Duchess of Malfi

Virginia Woolf
To the Lighthouse

W.B. Yeats
Selected Poems

Metaphysical Poets

GCSE and equivalent levels

Maya Angelou
I Know Why the Caged Bird Sings

Jane Austen
Pride and Prejudice

Alan Ayckbourn
Absent Friends

Elizabeth Barrett Browning
Select Poems

Robert Bolt
A Man for All Seasons

Harold Brighouse
Hobson's Choice

Charlotte Brontë
Jane Eyre

Emily Brontë
Wuthering Heights

Shelagh Delaney
A Taste of Honey

Charles Dickens
David Copperfield

Charles Dickens
Great Expectations

Charles Dickens
Hard Times

Charles Dickens
Oliver Twist

Roddy Doyle
Paddy Clarke Ha Ha Ha

George Eliot
Silas Marner

George Eliot
The Mill on the Floss

Anne Frank
The Diary of Anne Frank

William Golding
Lord of the Flies

Oliver Goldsmith
She Stoops to Conquer

Willis Hall
The Long and the Short and the Tall

Thomas Hardy
Far from the Madding Crowd

Thomas Hardy
The Mayor of Casterbridge

Thomas Hardy
Tess of the d'Urbervilles

Thomas Hardy
The Withered Arm and other Wessex Tales

L.P. Hartley
The Go-Between

Seamus Heaney
Selected Poems

Susan Hill
I'm the King of the Castle

Barry Hines
A Kestrel for a Knave

Louise Lawrence
Children of the Dust

Harper Lee
To Kill a Mockingbird

Laurie Lee
Cider with Rosie

Arthur Miller
The Crucible

Arthur Miller
A View from the Bridge

Robert O'Brien
Z for Zachariah

Frank O'Connor
My Oedipus Complex and Other Stories

George Orwell
Animal Farm

J.B. Priestley
An Inspector Calls

J.B. Priestley
When We Are Married

Willy Russell
Educating Rita

Willy Russell
Our Day Out

J.D. Salinger
The Catcher in the Rye

William Shakespeare
Henry IV Part 1

William Shakespeare
Henry V

William Shakespeare
Julius Caesar

William Shakespeare
Macbeth

William Shakespeare
The Merchant of Venice

William Shakespeare
A Midsummer Night's Dream

William Shakespeare
Much Ado About Nothing

William Shakespeare
Romeo and Juliet

William Shakespeare
The Tempest

William Shakespeare
Twelfth Night

George Bernard Shaw
Pygmalion

Mary Shelley
Frankenstein

R.C. Sherriff
Journey's End

Rukshana Smith
Salt on the Snow

John Steinbeck
Of Mice and Men

Robert Louis Stevenson
Dr Jekyll and Mr Hyde

Jonathan Swift
Gulliver's Travels

Robert Swindells
Daz 4 Zoe

Mildred D. Taylor
Roll of Thunder, Hear My Cry

Mark Twain
Huckleberry Finn

James Watson
Talking in Whispers

Edith Wharton
Ethan Frome

William Wordsworth
Selected Poems

A Choice of Poets

Mystery Stories of the Nineteenth Century including The Signalman

Nineteenth Century Short Stories

Poetry of the First World War

Six Women Poets